Hiring a Superstar!!!

Save Time and Money When Hiring Support Staff
for Your Small Business

Dr. Laura Shwaluk B.Sc., D.C.

Jerry Kezhaya A.A.M.

Published by Fun Stuff LLC
PO Box 940227
Plano, TX 75094

ISBN-10: 0-9797325-6-5

ISBN-13: 978-0-9797325-6-0

Contents

Disclaimer

Although the author and publisher have made every effort to ensure that the information in this book was correct at press time, the author and publisher do not assume and hereby disclaim any liability to any party for any loss, damage, or disruption caused by errors or omissions, whether such errors or omissions result from negligence, accident, or any other cause.

This book is not intended as a substitute for the legal advice of attorneys. The reader should consult an attorney in matters relating to legal matters, and particularly with respect to any matters pertaining to employment law.

As with any system involving humans, there are exceptions to the rules and guidelines. Try again, if at first you don't find the right person for the position.

In reading this book you understand that this is a guideline and that ultimately the responsibility of whom you hire rests on your shoulders 100%. We accept no responsibility or liability of any kind — nor does the publisher or any source or contributing author cited in this book — for whatever decisions you purportedly make as a result of something you read here.

Acknowledgements

The biggest acknowledgement goes to our Mastermind members. Your willingness to share with each other, grow yourselves personally, and hunker down to get the hard things done amazes and delights us to no end. Thank you for asking good questions and pushing us to be even better.

Special thanks to Cheryl Leo for proofreading this book and making fantastic suggestions.

Thank you also to all of the support people in our lives, without you no great success would be possible.

We would like to thank each other for always pushing to be better people and improving our relationship, as well as continuously supporting each other and saying words of encouragement. Most of all, we are grateful that after all these years, we still get a smile on our faces and a twinkle our eyes when we see each other.

Preface

The transformations you will get by implementing the steps from this book are:

1. Good people are easy to find with a system, and you can attract them easily while saving yourself time and money.

2. You can hire superstar employees!

As business owners we are always looking for ways to save time and money — hiring is no exception. If you own a business that requires hiring support staff, then you owe it to yourself to learn the time-saving shortcuts to hiring superstars for those positions.

This book is based on the hiring system we use in our businesses, which has been perfected over the past forty years of hiring and firing. This is not theory. This is what we use, as well as what we teach to our Business Builders Mentor and Mastermind clients. This is a proven system that takes you through the initial job description, hiring process, and what you may need to do if you need to fire someone. In addition to the hiring system you'll find stories of success and disaster, as well as wins and losses, in the hope that you will learn from our mistakes and insights and those of our Mastermind participants. There are helpful tips along the way and explanations of why each step is important.

We are not human resources experts. We are simply business owners with decades of experience that we want to share with you to make your hiring experience a WHOLE LOT EASIER, WHILE SAVING YOU TIME AND MONEY. As business owners all of us wear a lot of hats and are pulled in many directions. It is what we, knowingly or unknowingly, signed up for, so let's make it as easy on ourselves as possible.

Notes About This Book

1. Each section is written by Dr. Laura Shwaluk and Jerry Kezhaya unless a contributing author is specifically stated in the chapter or section.
2. Offers of additional resources from us appear in this book. You need not wait until you complete the book to take advantage of these opportunities and downloads.
3. Throughout the book you will encounter references to Business Builders Mentor and Mastermind. This is an organization dedicated to helping business owners implement the formulas and systems of successful businesses, so that they go from the struggle caused by not having enough time, money, or knowledge to having business success, maximum profit, AND the ability to take time off. Clients have access to several different online courses, weekly webinars, monthly Mastermind meetings, and access to us when they hit tough spots in their business and need someone to turn to for useful, implementable answers. If you would like to know more now, please visit www.BBMMUSA.com.

About the Authors

Dr Laura Shwaluk B.Sc, D.C.

Since 1996 Dr. Shwaluk has been practicing wellness and functional medicine in Texas where she incorporates nutrition, chiropractic, hormone balance, fitness and permanent weight control. Her Bachelor of Science in the field of Cellular, Molecular, and Microbial Biology is from the University of Calgary, Alberta, Canada. Her doctorate is in Chiropractic with certificates in neurology, applied kinesiology, nutrition and functional endocrinology. She is the author of wellness books "Take Charge" and "Reverse Type 2 Diabetes Forever." Her unique ability of delivering presentations in an upbeat and often humorous fashion, whether in a classroom setting or on TV, leaves her audiences with a new sense of excitement and motivation about increasing their health.

Laura is happily married and devoted to the love of her life, Jerry Kezhaya. Together they started Business Builders Mentor and Mastermind USA to help entrepreneurs accelerate their business and mindset growth. Her specialized business interests are in marketing, accounting, operational systems and especially kicking down the doors of people's mental blocks that are preventing them from succeeding.

Jerry Kezhaya A.A.M.

Jerry Kezhaya is originally from Detroit, Michigan and has called Plano Texas home since 1980. He started his first business, The Auto Shop, in 1981 and has grown to run several independent multimillion dollar businesses simultaneously. Jerry is a past recipient of the Small Business Person of the Year award of the city of Plano, Environmentalist of the year award for the state of Texas, Entrepreneur of the year for the State of Texas as well as *numerous* other awards displayed at The Auto Shop. Because Jerry has been successful, in both business and mentoring entrepreneurs, he has been sought after as a mentor for decades. He is humorous, willing to motivate people with his size 13W shoe up their backside, and has the ability to envision goals and needs far into the future to bring them into reality.

In addition to loving his wife, Jerry has two wonderful grown children and a wine hobby that has taken him to some of the most beautiful wine regions of the world. Jerry and Laura take 90 to 140 days each year to travel, learn and enjoy being with each other.

Both Jerry and Laura are available for a limited number of speaking engagements and new clients each year to Business Builders Mentor and Mastermind. They only accept clients who are truly committed to enormous growth and are genuinely nice people. Direct communication with Jerry and Laura can be accomplished by visiting www.BBMMUSA.com

About the Guest Contributors

Alex Cantaboni

Alessandro Cantaboni is Italian born and became an American citizen at age 24. He started Safe Pro Pest Control because he has a passion for helping people solve their pest control issues and felt like there was a way to provide pest control that would be better for the client, environment, and his employees. He has a commitment to learning and improving his mindset and business systems every day. The result is that he doubled his business, even while working fewer hours, in the first year he started with Business Builders Mentor and Mastermind.

Danielle Hasting

Danielle Hasting is the owner of One Fine Day, a Texas based event company specializing in logistical planning, event design and décor rentals for weddings, quinceañeras and corporate functions. Her team is rounded out by Certified Master Wedding

Planners, diligent office staff and creative assistants who make sure every detail of every event is handled professionally. She cannot think of anything more fun than working with families during one of the happiest times of their lives, and feels honored to be a part of the process of making the memories they will cherish forever. Danielle is committed to being the best event planner in the Dallas and Fort Worth Metroplex and has demonstrated her capacity for successful growth by taking her five year goal and making it reality within four months by being with Business Builders Mentor and Mastermind.

Aaron Miller

Aaron Miller is an elder law and estate planning attorney, accredited Veterans Administration benefits attorney, national speaker, and architect of the Family Defense System for which he has helped hundreds of people protect themselves and family. For the past three years, he has also helped train hundreds of attorneys across the country in elder law and estate planning. As the founder of the Miller Law Office, PLLC, he focuses exclusively on estate planning, probate, and elder law. Business Builders Mentor and Mastermind has helped him the most to be in action toward reaching his goals.

Jim Traister

Jim Traister is the CEO of HospitalityFan, a Social Media & Creative agency that drive sales via social media for independent businesses every day across the country. As a result of his team's work his clients have been featured on television, won contests and have been recognized by Yelp as one of the top 100 best at social media in the country. His social media teams have increased sales up to twenty percent for his clients. Jim is devoted to spending as much time as possible with his son, and strives to be the best role model possible in all aspects of life. The focus on the development of Standard Operating Procedures has been the biggest benefit he has received from Business Builders Mentor and Mastermind.

Chapter 1: Hiring a Superstar!

She was perfect. Just the person I thought I was looking for. The office staff person from heaven. Now I could really focus on the things I needed to do to run my business and not be concerned about the paperwork or answering the phones. Yay!

And then . . .

I noticed that she was often five to ten minutes late, would answer the phone while eating breakfast at her desk, and put on her makeup after she clocked in. She promised that she was detail oriented, but phone calls were not being returned, the schedule was off, and little piles of invoices and bills were strategically hidden and not being entered into the system.

Then I noticed that the little perks I usually received from vendors stopped coming in. So, I asked one specific vendor why they stopped sending me stuff? Was I suddenly a bad client? They said they hadn't stopped sending me fun things like cool shirts, yummy snacks, and other wonderful gifts. Was it the new hire? Yep, she showed up one day wearing the really cool shirt that the vendor had meant for me.

I hung my head as my shoulders slumped. I hated having to rely on employees. I wished I didn't have to hire anyone. And then the fantasy set in. . . .

Wouldn't it be nice to just sell stuff online and have no employees at all? It would be so wonderful! No W-2's, no time clocks, no enforcing the policies and procedures. No having to keep people accountable or fire anyone. Sigh.

Reality hit me like a punch in the gut.

Yeah, but then no cars would get repaired, no patients would get chiropractic adjustments, no pest control would get done, no roofs would be replaced, no beautifully executed weddings would get planned and executed, no food would be prepared or served in restaurants, and a zillion other things would never get done.

We needed employees.

Crap! I needed to find a better way to hire that would cut through people like this. I needed a way to *Hire a Superstar!*

Problems with Hiring

So many thousands of potential problems surround having employees. Some of them are real issues, like the risk of theft, or the possibility of workers not doing their jobs, not showing up when they say they will, or simply doing their jobs just well enough to not get fired, yet not well enough to be truly effective — a far cry from superstar status.

One of the challenges, as employers, is to get beyond our own mindset about employees. Many business owners get caught up in thinking any or all of the following:

(Put a check mark next to the ones you have experienced as true.)

- "Good people are hard to find."
- "I can't replace the people I have because they have worked for me so long."

14

- "People are lazy."
- "I can't afford to hire someone."
- "No one can do it like I do it."
- "If I want it done right, I gotta do it myself."
- "I can't fire them without repercussions."

Part of the goal of this book is to help you overcome those experiences and beliefs. Good people who want to work — superstar employees — really are out there.

Hiring can be time consuming!

Traditionally employers place an ad and then WASTE TIME waiting for replies, hoping for a "real" candidate. Then they WASTE MORE TIME sifting through emails and resumes, and WASTE EVEN MORE TIME setting up interviews to which the majority of people don't even show up!

It can be a VERY frustrating process.

This system will SIGNIFICANTLY cut your wasted time AND help you find superstar employees.

This hiring process allows you to weed through many candidates, basically through the process of elimination, so that you end up with just a few of the "cream of the crop" and best qualified. As a part of this system candidates must jump through several hoops that, if not completed, will automatically disqualify them. This will prevent you from wasting time reading hundreds of resumes and having one-on-one interviews with unqualified candidates.

Once this system is set up, it will be very easy to find superstar employees at any time for multiple support staff positions.

Why Do We Hire People?

The common answer to "Why do we hire people?" is: to do a job. But that isn't totally true. As an employer, **you hire someone to do the things you *can't* do or the things you no longer *want* to do.**

Your job is to find the *right* one for the position. To do this you must take your emotions and desperation (for a warm body in the position) out of the equation and use a system.

Contribution from Aaron Miller

One of the biggest benefits you've got from hiring people and having support staff: It's leveraging your time, easily. They can do things that either I don't like to do or I can't get to. Even though . . . it is possible I do it better. But if I don't have to do it, I can work on the things that only I can work on. Whether that's meeting with clients or doing the high-level legal work or doing the high-level business work. The biggest and greatest thing is having somebody else who can handle all that stuff for me, and when they're not there, it really hurts.

Four Important Traits of Superstar Employees

#1 Attitude
Superstar performance starts with attitude and shows up in behavior, which produces results. It has little to do with having an ability to do the job. In fact, it is often great to start with someone who does not know anything about the position, yet has a super attitude toward learning and getting things done right. At the heart of every superstar employee is a natural motivation toward the type of work that helps them keep up their attitude. They really enjoy what they do, which drives them

toward performing to the highest level possible. Nobody can perform to the high standards that superstar employees do if they don't **love their chosen profession**. People who undertake jobs that they don't really want to do will achieve mediocre results.

Attitude isn't something that can be "managed," "inspired," or "trained" into people. They either have it or they don't. It is intrinsically built into them as a result of their upbringing.

So, since superstar employees start with a good attitude and are self-motivated, you must ensure that they don't become de-motivated by *your* leadership or other employees.

#2 Commitment
Superstar employees care about the company they work for, and they behave as if they are an owner of the company. They take their responsibilities and the company viability seriously!

They will usually give an employer a decent length of service before seeking new pastures, often putting up with career plateaus for a short time to see if things start to move again. Things have got to be pretty bad before they pick up and leave. This does not mean you can take them for granted. In fact, appreciation and acknowledgement will go a long way to keeping them in place.

#3 Determination
Everybody experiences stress, failures, and setbacks, but superstars don't let these diversions get them down and have a negative impact on their performance. They pick themselves up, dust themselves off, and get on with the job at hand. They are steadfast at taking action on a project until they get the desired outcome.

You can usually count on the fact that they gave you their word; however, it is always good to have projects and procedures in writing and check up on them to ensure they are making progress. The last thing any team needs is a "flake" or someone who crumbles under pressure! So you must *inspect* their work to be sure that you get what you *expect*.

#4 Tolerance
Superstar employees don't job hop. So, unless the workplace is really intolerable, they keep going toward their career goal and don't let anything knock them off course.

They know it is not a good idea to change jobs every six to twelve or eighteen months, and get labeled a "job hopper."

Obviously, if they have picked up the experience they are after and career progression is limited with their employer, then they may move on to keep moving up, but that is not likely to happen until eighteen to twenty-four months into their employment at the minimum.

There are potential superstar employees out there today, who, despite your fantastic program of incentives and benefits, are highly self-motivated to climb up the ladder. So be prepared to *always be hiring*.

You *can* attract them to your company!

Do You Have the Right Number of Positions?

Before you hire anyone, it may be time to assess the employee positions in your company. This short section answers the question, "Do I have enough people *or* too many people in my business?"

The most common positions in a service-based business are:
1. Support Staff (see list below)
2. Salespeople
3. People to Provide the Actual Service or Product

Additional positions as you grow:
1. General Manager or Operational Manager
2. Bookkeeper/Accountant
3. Sales Manager
4. Marketer
5. IT Personnel
6. Inventory and Supply Manager
7. Human Resources Manager

It may be helpful to create an organizational chart showing which duties are assumed under which job title. Then you can really see on paper whether you have the right number of positions.

Hiring Support Staff

This book focuses on hiring superstar support staff. These are the people who keep an organization running and *support* the people who are involved in the organization's main business. In a start-up small business the following positions may all be done by one person:
1. Office Administrator
2. Customer Service Representative(first customer contact/ who answers the phones)
3. Scheduling/Dispatch
4. Data Entry personnel

A general rule is that as your business grows to over $500,000 in gross annual sales, you will likely need to fill all four support staff positions, especially as you reach the $1 million mark in gross annual sales.

NOTE: This may vary depending on the business and how effectively your systems are implemented. You can find out more about effective, time-saving and money-saving systems in the Systems Module at www.BBMMUSA.com.

How Expensive Is It to Hire the Wrong Person?

Have you ever thought about what it would cost you to make the wrong hiring decision? Here is an example:

1. Recruiting Cost (10% of annual salary)	$3,000
2. Training Cost	$10,000
3. Salary Cost/Year	$30,000
4. Bad Performance Cost	$100,000
5. Management Time Cost	$50,000
6. Pollute Your Culture (bad work climate)	<u>$100,000</u>
	$293,000/year

A bad salesperson can cost you $500,000, and that does not even include revenue from lost sales.

Here is a statistic from the *Harvard Business Review*: **Eighty percent of employee turnover is the result of bad hiring decisions.**

Nine Big Mistakes Employers Make When Hiring

1. Hiring too quickly — hire SLOW, fire FAST.
2. Hiring on gut feelings — people can be deceiving.
3. Acting on recommendation from others — other people don't know your needs.
4. Accepting references from previous employers at face value — they are legally limited in what they can say.
5. Relying on an aced interview — anyone can be great for an hour.
6. Giving too much weight to testing well — e.g., their personality or IQ Test score was great.

7. Requiring an impressive resume — they may have skill, but do they have the will to do the job?
8. Choosing the candidate based solely on their enthusiasm— the person with the highest energy in the interview is not always the best person for the job.
9. Taking someone on because you have so much in common with the applicant — this is definitely NOT a criteria for hiring someone; you are not hiring people to be your friends or to have someone to hang out with.

Most hiring decisions are based on enthusiasm and whether the employer likes the applicant. Slow down, don't be desperate. Just because someone can "fog a mirror" (they are a live human being) and they say they want to work for you does not mean you should hire them.

Do You Have the Right People?

Changing your staff is a tough decision and usually a very difficult and painful one. However, the reality is that team members who are resistant to improving and developing are typically not good for your business and will often undermine rather than reinforce the company attitude. You could see this as an opportunity to replace them with people who are more flexible and more willing to embrace change. People problems rarely solve themselves, so take action.

Hire slow, fire fast!

In the words of Jim Collins, **"If you can't change your people, change your people!"**

How do you know if you have the right people working for you?

The answer comes in the form of several different questions to ask yourself:

- Is there anyone who is dragging my company down or sucks the life out of me?
- Am I continuing to pay someone even though they are not doing their job or I don't trust them?
- Do I feel obligated to keep someone even though I should let them go?
- Are they making the same mistakes, even after being trained and retrained?
- Are they NOT open to learning new things or accepting change?
- Am I waking up in the night angry or frustrated with any of my employees?
- Is there an employee on my mind just before bedtime, as I doze off, or when I wake up in the morning?

If someone's name popped into your mind, write their name(s) here.

The answer to "Do I have the right people?" also comes in the form of asking your customers:
- How would they rate my support staff?
- If they had a position open, would they want to hire my people?
- Is there anyone in my business my customers try to avoid or complain about?

Contribution from Aaron Miller

I had been told I needed to fire her for a long time, but didn't want to and couldn't bring myself to cut her loose. Nostalgia was one part of the equation. . . . She was the daughter of the lady that was in the position before her. It really wasn't

22

intended to be too long of a job because at the time I was kind of scaling things back.

I didn't really need somebody to do a whole lot. But as I changed direction again and I needed her more and more, she just wasn't able to keep up. She was sick a lot and so she worked out of her house.

She did not come to the office for most of the time, and that was okay, because I didn't have a physical office at the time. I would meet clients at an office space, but that's not where she did her work or I did my work. She was set up for an easy position.

The problem with her working from home was that I couldn't really monitor what she was doing. I would ask her to do something, and I wasn't always sure it got done.

Basically, her primary job was to make appointments for me and deal with emails, answer the phones, return calls to people, and things like that. Sometimes these things got done, sometimes they didn't get done.

I knew she was having problems with getting stuff done and keeping track of my schedule. There was one time, I remember, where I had two or three appointments back to back. Which was great except there was somebody else that was waiting in the lobby and I didn't find out until the day was over that he was waiting for me.

That happened a couple times, and then there were other times where she put an appointment on my calendar but hadn't confirmed it with the client yet. So I'd show up to a meeting the client didn't know anything about.

The cost of these mistakes can be enormous, both with revenue and reputation. There is one particular case that usually, when I get those cases and based on the numbers, it would bring in $3,000 per case. She got the schedule wrong three times in two days and it cost me $9,000 in lost revenue— **$9,000 IN TWO DAYS!**

That was not fun. Then, basically, working with Jerry Kezhaya, he was like, "Listen, you got to let her go."

It was a fairly painful process just because, like I said, she was the daughter of the lady that worked for me before. I was friends with that lady, and to an extent, friends with her as well.

I guess I'm a highly sympathetic person as it goes, anyway, so it was painful for me. What I said to her was: "Look, I need someone who can do the job. I think we both realize that you can't." At that point I'd already hired her replacement, which made it a little easier, but it was still tough.

Right after the phone call where I fired her, I was kind of bummed and stressed out, because that was a difficult call for me to make. However, it was a much better decision for the business. It was definitely the right call, because I found somebody who my clients call "the crown jewel of our office." They love talking with her and she pays attention to all the details and follows the systems we have set up to make everything flow easily and successfully.

For the business, it was a much better decision and I wish I had hired her sooner. She actually works full time in the office with me now. I don't have a virtual person doing that anymore. It's a lot easier to know exactly what she's doing because I can just ask her —she's right there.

If there are people who keep coming to mind while reading this section, it is time to replace them with superstars.

The agreement with your employees is this: "Here's your list of things I need you to do, and in return I will pay you this much money."

If they don't do that list of things, why are you still paying them? Why are you still giving them YOUR money when they are not giving you what you both agreed to?

Now, does any part of that sound unreasonable? The soft squishy part that says, "Oh, I want to love everybody and I want everyone to love me."

Here's what you need to really get: **They are taking your money and ruining your reputation.** These underperforming people are taking food from your children. They're taking vacation time from your family. They're taking vacation money that they didn't deserve. They're taking things away from you, your family, and your life.

This is NOT like a teacher and student situation, where 50% or 80% of the work done passes them to the next level. No, 80% is no longer good enough. They have to do their job 100% or they don't get paid.

That's part of the issue with people who are used to getting a grade in school rather than a paycheck for performance. There are some things students simply choose not to do on purpose because they don't feel like doing them. But that's no longer the case when it comes to the real world and having a job.

When employees are underperforming, they needed to be written up. Seriously. You write them up, and you write them up a second time, a third time, and then say, "Thank you very much for playing. Now get off my property."

I had a guy just like this working in my parts department. His direct supervisor told him, "There are seven catalytic converters that are in the trash. We need you to pull those out so that we can recycle them for money." The employee went and got three of them and then told one of the technicians, "F— this shit. I ain't doing this. I'm out." He then went back into the parts department and sat down at his desk.

The technician told me about it, and so I called the parts guy to my office. He came into my office wearing his uniform and his name badge, and I said, "Come talk to me." I said, "Tell me what happened about the converters."

He said, "What? I did part of it."

I said, "Oh, but you want a full paycheck, right?"

To which he replied, "Well, yeah."

I said, "Well, you don't get a full paycheck for only doing part of the work that you were told to do."

He said, "Are you shittin' me?"

"No, let's just call this done." And I took his name tag off and I said, "Your paycheck will be ready next Thursday, and make sure you turn in all your uniforms or the cost of the uniforms will be removed from your paycheck."

He looked shocked and said, "You're firing me?"

My reply was, "Did you do the job you were told to do?"

"Well, no I didn't," he admitted.

"There you go. Yes, I am firing you. Good-bye."

In total disbelief, "You're firing me 'cause I didn't do what you told me to do?"

"Yeah, that's how it works in the real world, son. Those converters cost a lot of money. You put them in the trash and wouldn't get them out. Now, the trash truck came and picked them up so we can't get them back. You cost me a lot of money. You can't do that and still expect to keep your job and get paid."

The reason people don't fire their employees is that they don't want to deal with confrontation. As an employer, you don't want to be the bad guy. So I'd like you to reframe it: **What you're doing is bringing to their attention that they're the bad guy**. You, or their supervisor, told them to do something, which was specific and direct, and they knew what they needed to do.

And did they do that? NO!

In no uncertain terms they "flipped you off" and said, "I'll take your money but I ain't doing jack for you." Who's going to put up with that? No good business owner would put up with that. You have to set a precedent. You have to cut that one, and all the rest of the employees will take note.

You don't give employees a trophy or ribbon just for showing up. You get a trophy for doing something, and the trophy's called a paycheck. If they're not willing to do the work, you are keeping the trophy, which is the paycheck!

Look, you can be as kindhearted as you can afford. I know I'm making it sound simple, yet it may seem difficult because a lot of emotion is involved, but at the same time it *is* simple.

I want you to imagine an amazing balancing act. You can think of it like a seesaw or teeter-totter, or a set of balance scales. On one side is intelligence and on the other is emotion. When emotions go up, intelligence always goes down.

They have written books and made movies about this. It is called "crimes of passion." People go to jail for crimes of passion. For example: "Man, I was crazy about that girl . . . "

Try to keep the emotion out of it, as much as you can, and be smart with your money and your business. We all would love to pay people and be the nice guy, but we can't. Hell, I went into the shop one day and found a guy working out with my weights on my clock. That happened only once.

But it happened. And you have to be prepared to do or say whatever you need to so that kind of thing no longer happens.

Listen, at the end of the day people are people. We all want to do the easiest thing. You've got to be self-disciplined as an employer. You know that your business and everybody else's livelihood depends on your doing not only the right thing, but everything, even when you don't want to or don't feel like it. Man, the show must go on. The public doesn't care what is going on behind the scenes in your company.

When your employees don't do their job, you have to be there to clean up the mess. I guarantee you it's a hell of a lot harder, it's a hell of a lot more expensive, and it's a hell of a lot more time consuming to clean up a mess than it is to prevent one. We all know that.

Contribution from Danielle Hasting

Poor performance sullies your reputation. It reduces the chance of getting referrals. Yeah, it's a bad thing. So now ask yourself again, how lenient should you be? I'm an asshole on the little things. See, I want the little things to be done perfectly so we create the space for the great things to happen naturally. But if you don't have the little things in place, great things can never happen. They can't.

You have to have everybody so habitual, their habit has to be to do good things all the time. To do the little things greatly, all the time. So when they're doing the little things, they have that down to a science big stuff just happens.

That's really where you are setting the foundation. Then you need to get them to understand the big picture and where they fit in and how they make a huge difference.

You have to acknowledge them by saying things like, "Hey, come here. Give me a minute. I really like what you did there. That was really great, and if you really want to kick it out of the park next time, here's a way you can do it even better." But for you to go in and only scold them . . . people don't take scolding well. Emotions rise and their attitude ends with, "Ah, screw you, I'm outta here."

The Work Culture

Here's the thing that we all seem to run into: We all want to be liked. And we all want to be liked by everybody. And even more we want to like all of our employees, we want to be their friend. Right?

I mean, we want them to say, "Hey, how you doing, boss?" when you walk in the room, not "grumble, grumble, grumble." Or worse yet, ignore you.

Do not let the need to be liked cause you to be tolerant of poor performance or bad attitudes from your employees. When my employees come up to me and ask me something silly like,

"Where's the coffee creamer?" I tell my people, "I cannot imagine somebody walking up to Steve Jobs when he was president of Apple and asking him that question." Ever read anything about Steve Jobs? He was a tyrant. If he didn't like your design and you were making a presentation, he would fire you in front of everybody, tell you to get your shit out of his building. Screaming at you about what a piece of shit you were. But the work culture was all about making sure the little things, the details, were perfect.

That's the culture. And that's how it is at Amazon, and that's how it is at Zappos, and that's how it is at all of the really successful companies. Elon Musk of Tesla is a tyrant, absolute tyrant, except when he's onstage. That's when he's selling. It's okay — I dig it. And people love working for Tesla, and they love working for Apple.

We think we're doing a service to our people by letting the little things slide. When the reality of it is, letting the little things slide is killing our companies. And it's actually counterproductive to the long-term goal and mission of your company.

CEO Tasks

What is the role of the business owner (CEO)? As the business owner, HOW you are in this role will define the success of your company.

Here is a list of what your role includes:

1. **Be the Leader** — Share your vision and keep your finger on the pulse of your business.
2. **Think** — Good CEOs have good ideas that can build an organization. They solve problems and are never at the

mercy of ruthless people who would take advantage of them or try to deceive them.

3. **Show Courage** — This may mean that you are the one who decides when and how to fire someone.

4. **Know Your Numbers** — Get the pricing right and make sure everyone knows the "score." Is the business meeting the projected goals? All employees need to know if they and the company are winning or losing.

5. **Brainstorm Strategies, Goals and Solutions** — Do this with your Mastermind group and key employees.

6. **Listen to Your Customers** — This helps you see into the future of what they need and want, and question popular thinking.

7. **Steer the Ship** — Tell people what to do and hold them accountable.

8. **Spearhead Marketing** — No one knows your company like you do. Do not leave this to chance or an advertising agency.

9. **Read** — Constantly improve yourself and take in new ideas.

10. **Hold Meetings** – Meet frequently with your key employees, customers, and prospects.

In the reference section at the back of this book you will find links to great articles on how the best CEOs spend their time.

Be Prepared to Lose Your Employees

Owning a business is not for the faint of heart. So, as your business grows, you may lose some employees who are not able to grow with you. Some employees are afraid to grow; others don't like change. Among them a few might fear that their "territory" will be taken from them. You will have employees that will do anything to protect their little "fiefdom" within your kingdom.

Being a business owner is tough. It's tough all by itself. Now, when you add someone like us as your mentor, pushing you to grow and change because we can see the potential that you can't see or can't figure out how to achieve, it can be a lot for you and your employees to handle.

Less than 1% of Americans even think to start a business, much less take it on. So that means 99% of the people in your world think that owning a business is so radical! Others can't even see it. I mean, it's not even in their scope of vision, much less their scope of possibility.

Understand that the people you have working for you are in that 99% mentality. When you have your company meetings, you must start pulling them into *your* world. The cream will rise to the top, and the rest of them will go away. Don't be concerned about high turnover at first. I always have a certain form on my desk: It is a Voluntary Resignation form with a "fill in the blank" for their name. (The voluntary resignation form is included in the downloads at www.BBMMUSA.com/p/Hiring) You need to understand: Not everybody is okay with doing what you do or the way you do it. You can't make them wrong for that — you just replace them as fast as possible with superstars!

Do not be afraid of replacing EVERYONE. You have to build your team your way, and they have to get your culture.

Contribution from Jim Traister

Some of the mottos that I live by in our hiring process come from one of my mentors, Don Smith. One of the key phrases or mottos he utilized is, ***"Don't hire ducks to go to eagle school."*** If you were to ask him, "What does that mean?" Essentially it's, if you're looking for eagles who are going to soar, don't hire a duck. If you're going to train them to be eagles, or if you're looking for eagles, don't hire ducks.

So, maybe it's hiring them from a competitor . . . or maybe it's a certain level of experience that they already have and have demonstrated through their results.

The second hiring motto I do my best to live by is, *"Hire fast, fire faster."*

At the end of the day, I really believe hiring is subjective. If you've done hiring before, no matter how many tests somebody goes through, all of a sudden they may show up to a job, and they're just not eligible to join your team for long-term. In that case it's important to fire faster. For me, my intuition tells me that I have to trust that the standards are being met, but if they just don't feel like a good fit, I don't start justifying, perhaps telling myself, "Hey, maybe it's this, or give them the benefit of the doubt." Like I've said to one of my supervisors, "They haven't earned that benefit of the doubt yet as far as I'm concerned." Especially since the beginning of their employment is when they're going to be on their best behavior!

My third motto from Mr. Smith is, *"The same exact team that plays in the Super Bowl this year is not the same one that plays next year."* I had to ask him, what did he mean by that? His point was, even if a team wins the Super Bowl, they're still hiring for the next year, and new people are going to be replacing others on the team. He always talked about lopping off the bottom. Some people think that's a little harsh, but that's the reality of any sports team. I like to think that we coach or we manage like a sports team. Not everybody is going to be capable of playing the next year on our team, without question. We're always hiring.

What Can You Delegate?

Business owners get exhausted, burned out, and sloppy when they are doing tasks that could be delegated. The business owner's time is the most valuable.

Let's look at your TIME and your TEAM.

You need to spend your time doing the things that make the biggest impact on your business's bottom line and delegate the tasks that are low impact. Would the CEO of a large corporation do a $10 per hour task? No, of course not. In order to grow your business and achieve the freedom you desire, you MUST delegate the low wage per hour tasks.

Complete the following exercise and start delegating! Do this exercise now. Do not jump ahead. It should take you ten to fifteen minutes to complete.

"The best way to build a business bigger than you is delegating." — **Dave Ramsey**

Delegating Exercise

STEP 1: Take out two fresh sheets of paper, and on one sheet write down ALL the things you do during the day that drain you of energy or are tasks that can be done by someone whom you could pay minimum wage. On the other sheet of paper write down ALL the things you do that build your energy or the tasks required of the CEO.

HINT: The things that move you forward toward your goals are usually the things that build your energy, and the things that take you farther from your goals are commonly the things that drain you of energy. Here is an example:

34

DRAINS my energy:
- data entry
- cleaning
- answering the phone

BUILDS my energy:
- meeting with my team to implement systems
- creating a new product or service
- brainstorming with my employees

STEP 2: Put a capital *D* next to the items that you can delegate right away to someone you currently employ.

STEP 3: Put a capital *N* next to the items that you need to hire a new employee to complete.

STEP 4: Delegate the tasks you put a *D* next to — as quickly as possible.

When you have the right people in the right places and you free yourself up to tackle the things a good CEO provides, you will have a VERY successful business that will have consistent growth.

Chapter 2: Hiring System Part 1

STEP 1: Complete Job Description

The first step of the hiring process focuses on the job analysis. This becomes the basis for developing a concise job description. Some of the following information about job descriptions may be found on the PrimePay website. Please see the Resources section of the appendix at the back of this book for the complete link.

A well-written job description is critical for ensuring your employees understand the responsibilities and requirements of each particular job. It is also a key resource to help you review employee performance, hire employees, develop recruitment advertising, and make sure your compensation is competitive so you can attract the most qualified candidates.

When developing a job description, be sure you do not violate disability nondiscrimination laws such as the Americans with Disabilities Act. Compliance guidance is available from the Office of Disability Employment Policy and the Job Accommodation Network (JAN). For more information on recruiting and hiring people with disabilities, please review the Recruiting & Hiring section on Disability.gov.

Nine Core Elements for Developing a Good, Concise Job Description

1. Job Summary Overview

A summary overview is a brief outline of a job's purpose and goals and should be about three or four sentences. The specific job description details, such as tasks and experience, will be covered in the remaining parts of the job description.

2. General Information

- Job title and classification: The job title should be concise (i.e., Web Developer). Be sure to indicate whether the job is exempt or nonexempt under the Fair Labor Standards Act.
- Workplace location.
- Management/reporting responsibilities: Identify to whom this position reports and where this position fits on the company organizational chart.

3. Tasks

- Identify no more than 10 tasks. For example: managing accounts payable, managing payroll administration. Be as concise as possible, and try to keep the task descriptions to one line each. Be sure to also include a basic statement that communicates other responsibilities that may be required within the scope of this position.
- The tasks should be organized in a logical manner. Begin each task description with an action verb such as *develop, organize, manage, create, oversee,* or *coordinate*.
- When describing each task, include the benefit of the task when possible. For example: "Update marketing database to ensure all client information is current."

4. Skills

- Identify the skills, expertise, and knowledge base necessary to perform each task listed in the job description.
- Describe any special skills that require additional training, certification, etc.

5. Experience

- Identify relevant past experience required.
- Include any special professional certifications that may be required.
- Include any special education requirements.

6. **Work Conditions**
   - Work hours.
   - Travel requirements.
   - Unusual environmental conditions.

7. **Compensation**
   - Pay range and benefits information.
   - Bonuses and any other incentives.

8. **Company Description**

Include a description of the company as well. You want to sell the candidates on working for your company, so it is important to make a great first impression.

9. **Disclaimers**

A disclaimer can typically be placed at the end of the job description to provide flexibility in adding or changing job responsibilities. The following is an example of this type of disclaimer: "This job description may be changed to include new responsibilities and tasks or modify existing ones as management deems necessary."

10. **Periodic Review of Job Descriptions**

It's a good idea to review job descriptions on a regular basis as the tasks, responsibilities, and requirements may change. In addition, you want to make sure you have realistic expectations about the jobs being performed.

Contribution from Jim Traister

The first thing is to know what you're looking for, and I believe that starts off with a job description. This is important to know because if you're not exactly sure of the skill set you're looking for, you're just shooting at multiple targets, and that just doesn't make sense.

Then, number two is what hours? Understand the hours that you want them to work. If you're a restaurant, are you hiring for the night shift? Day shift? Both? It's understanding their availability as well too, right? In our case, people just have to be very flexible with their hours. That's the second criteria defined.

Also, start date. Maybe they're not capable of starting next week. I've made this mistake before. For example, finding out they're going on a vacation the next week and a half. It really sucks when I come to learn I've already offered a job to someone before I've asked them, "Hey, do you have any vacations planned or are you going to be available for this date?" In my mind, if I was to hire somebody, I'm ready for them to start with training for a week and a half, not have vacation time. So now, I always ask if people can be available during a period of time. For me, it's the first three months without vacation. Are you available to work that entire time? I don't start training if that time period is going to be interrupted — just from the mistakes I've made in the past.

The following is a clear example of a job description. You can save yourself some time by downloading this description and tweaking it for your own use. Visit our website www.BBMMUSA.com/p/Hiring to get the free download of this job description.

Example of Job Description

Marketing Coordinator/Lead Coordinator

The role of the Lead Coordinator is to make initial contact with prospects who have responded to some form of marketing media, such as direct mail, television/radio commercials, or online marketing. Following a script, the Lead Coordinator makes contact with a prospective client with the intentions of setting and confirming their attendance at one of the free seminars on health that we offer. From that point they follow the client and keep track of statistics on who showed up for the seminar, signed up for a consultation with the doctor, and purchased a health program.

The Lead Coordinator plays a critical role in the sales process by becoming the first point of human contact between the company and the customer. This person makes sure that each prospect has a very smooth experience in their transition from **simple interest to "WOW, I want to be a client here."**

Responsibilities:
- Making initial telephone contact with our prospects.
- Setting and tracking which seminar the prospect is interested in attending.
- Following a scripted process to facilitate the conversion from prospect to client.
- Keeping records in each category of marketing media of calls completed, seminar attendance, and conversion to client, as well as money spent on media and what clients spend with us.
- Entering information on company forms and computer systems.
- Completing other administrative duties as required by the business.
- Helping to coordinate marketing materials.
- Answering/placing phone calls — when clients first call or email, to confirm and to follow up.
- Executing accurate data entry and keeping track of conversion rate statistics.
- Going to get the food for the seminars and setting it out the day of the seminar.
- Making sure we have the printed marketing materials.
- Running errands to the post office, Costco, Kroger, Office Max, or print shop.
- Helping with front desk scheduling, data entry, and money collection.
- Keeping track of daily, weekly, and monthly statistics.
- Giving new-patient tours of the office.
- Providing patient support — field questions and act as doctor-patient correspondent.
- Demonstrating community involvement — attend luncheons, expos, volunteer events.
- Following up to make sure that clients are having a great experience.

Qualifications:
- Excellent communications and customer service skills are required.
- Strong persuasion and influencing skills are desired.
- A positive attitude and the ability to build relationships are a must.
- The ability to flex and learn new processes along with strict attention to details are needed.
- Basic computer skills are necessary, particularly Microsoft Word and Excel.

Professional dress code: skirts/slacks, blouses, dress shoes (no scrubs or tennis shoes)

Office hours: Monday to Thursday hours are 8:15AM to approximately 6:00PM (until daily tasks are done).
1 hour for lunch
One evening each week is seminar night, so working as late as 9:00 PM.

Pay structure: $10–$14/hour, plus bonuses. No insurance benefits. No direct deposit. Paid every 2 weeks.

What qualifies you for this position: We are looking for someone who is an upbeat, confident, intelligent, and pleasant team player with enthusiasm without being rushed. This person MUST be detail oriented to handle statistics and enjoy talking with people to lead them through a process efficiently.

What disqualifies you for this position: If you like drama or gossip or a messy environment, this job is not for you. If you find it difficult to talk to people or don't care about people, you need not apply. Some of our clients come in feeling terrible (sick and depressed), so we must be considerate of them.

We need someone who has a "can do" attitude with a smile on their face, who will jump in, figure things out, and make things happen.

STEP 2: Job Ad Description

This is the job ad that potential employees will see when searching for a job. It is shorter and more concise than the complete job description.

The following is a clear example of a job advertisement. You can download this ad for your own use by visiting our website www.BBMMUSA.com/p/Hiring .

Example of Job Ad

Front Desk Lead Coordinator

The role of the Front Desk Lead Coordinator is to make initial contact with prospects who have responded to our marketing media. This person plays a critical role in the process by being the first point of human contact between the company and the customer, and makes sure that each prospect has a very smooth experience.

For an interview, please call (____) ____-_____ and leave a message. DO NOT EMAIL.

Responsibilities:
• Return phone calls and emails from prospects.
• Follow a scripted process to facilitate the conversion from prospect to client.
• Help coordinate marketing materials.
• Execute accurate data entry and keep track of conversion rate statistics.
• Help with front desk scheduling, data entry, money collection.
• Give new-patient tours of the office.
• Providing patient support — field questions and act as doctor-patient correspondent.
• Demonstrate community involvement —attend luncheons, expos, volunteer events.
• Follow up to make sure that clients are having a great experience.

Qualifications:
• Excellent communications and customer service skills are required.
• Strong persuasion and influencing skills are desired.
• A positive attitude and the ability to build relationships are a must.
• Basic computer skills are necessary, particularly Microsoft Word and Excel.

Professional dress code: skirts/slacks, blouses, dress shoes
Office hours: Monday to Thursday 8:15AM to approximately 6:00PM (until daily tasks are done), and one evening each week working as late as 9:00PM for seminar night (usually Tuesday or Thursday).

Pay structure: $10–$14/hour, plus bonus.

DO NOT EMAIL. For an interview, please call (____) ____-_____ and leave a message.

Contribution from Aaron Miller

We followed the hiring process that you guys teach. But we made a big mistake and learned that we need to be really clear in the ad. We put a couple of ads out there, and we put the hourly rate in the headline, but we didn't put it in the body of the ad.

We had a lady come in for an interview from a big law firm with a lot of great credentials. Somehow or another, we asked her what her salary expectations were, and she gave a number that was triple per year what it said in the job ad headline. The interview quickly stopped after that.

So, make it clear. In fact, probably have somebody else read through the ad and then ask them about the major parts, just to make sure that the ad is easy to understand and your intentions are clear.

STEP 3: Outgoing Message

Set up a dedicated voice mailbox that will enable you to record an outgoing message and give applicants the opportunity to leave messages for you. We highly recommend an online voicemail system for this, rather than a physical machine. Online accounts give you the freedom to listen to messages from any computer and not use your cell phone minutes.

This step is VERY important, because it gives you the opportunity to listen to each person's message and weed out people who would not be a fit for the position. This is the secret to cutting through stacks of resumes and preventing yourself from getting into trouble with discrimination laws.

The outgoing message should explain about the position, such as duties, what kind of attitude you're looking for, what you're not looking for, and the kind of atmosphere you have in your business — positive things about your office like, "friendly, family oriented, no drama, " etc. You want this to make applicants confident and excited about the position. You can use the sample hiring script below, making appropriate changes to fit your office, but stick with the basic script because it works.

The following is a clear example of the hiring outgoing message. Download this description for your own use by visiting our website www.BBMMUSA.com/p/Hiring .

EXAMPLE SCRIPT

Hello, you've reached the voice mailbox for the NTC Health and Fitness job postings. My name is Dr. Laura Shwaluk, the owner of NTC Health and Fitness, and I wanted to tell you a little bit more about us and this job before you leave a message. First of all, I want you to know that I know how tough it can be to find that "just-right job" when you're searching through tons of postings and maybe even going through tons of interviews that are not at all what you expected. I can tell you: This is a real job that pays real money. This is not network marketing. We are a small business, but by no means are we a fly-by-night, so you don't have to worry about that. We are a successful, busy, and always growing wellness center in the Plano/Richardson area. We are looking to hire as soon as possible, hopefully within the next two weeks. So, I'll tell you a little bit more about this particular position. There are currently two doctors in our practice: I am one of them, and the other is Dr. Asby. Both of us are chiropractors who specialize in functional medicine. Now, you may not know what that is, and that's quite alright. You can look it up. But, basically we deal with the underlying cause of a disease and work with the body to help regain normal function in a natural way, without the use of harmful drugs or surgery if they can be avoided. In a nutshell, it's alternative medicine. Because of this, this is a very rewarding work environment because we're literally helping to change people's lives. That is why it is so important that the person we hire for this position must really care about other people and have an attitude of service. Our patients often tell us that our office is the most fun and positive place they visit all week, and that is completely on purpose on our part. We do our best to create that experience for them the minute they walk through our doors. We do not have a big staff, so it is very much like a work family environment. Everyone genuinely likes each other and gets along well even if we don't agree with each other. Again, this is completely on purpose. We hire only people who are team players and have the strongest of work ethics, so that we can depend on each other and trust one another to do our jobs. Because we are a wellness center and are focused on health, anyone we hire must have an interest in and actively take care of themselves. This doesn't mean you have to be a fitness model or be a perfect physical specimen; it just means that you have to believe in being proactive in taking care of yourself and that you look and feel as healthy as our patients want to. We have to practice what we preach to our patients. So, let me tell you a few things that would definitely disqualify you for this position. If you like to whine and complain about things, this job is not for you, as we have to have people with a can-do attitude. If you really do not like people or do not care about helping people, then do not apply. You would be dealing with all sorts of people; some of them are sick and depressed, so you have to be caring and compassionate. If you are very shy, it will be a problem. You really need to be outgoing. If you don't care about your health or your physical appearance, or if you are sick all the time, do not apply. If you are not a detail-oriented person, please do not apply for this position. Details need to be something you enjoy.

So, after listening to this message you feel like you still would like this job, please leave a brief message with your first and last name and best contact number. I will be returning calls to those I feel are possible candidates throughout this coming week and weekend, and I wish you all the best of luck in your job search!

STEP 4: Place Your Job Ad

Two of the easiest sites for posting job ads are Craigslist and Indeed.com. It is simple to create your accounts and cut and paste your already-made job ad into these sites.

Depending on the area in which you live, there may or may not be a fee for Craigslist.

Indeed gives you the choice to list your ad for free or pay for more people to see the job ad. We always choose free and it works quite well. Note that many people will still email their resume to you anyway via Indeed. You can simply reply back in the Indeed internal email system to call the number if they are interested in the position.

We have found that placing the ad in the midafternoon on Monday, Tuesday, or Wednesday works best. This will save you time by weeding out the people who are not working and are spending their morning sending resumes out just to satisfy their unemployment requirements. This may also help increase the number of applicants looking for a real job, rather than later in the week when they would rather be looking for ideas for weekend entertainment.

STEP 5: Listen to the Messages

This step is where you hear the actual voices of the applicants. I love this step, as it allows you to pick and choose quickly and easily the voice you may hire to answer your phones and interact with your customers. If done properly, you can go through over one hundred applicants in less than fifteen minutes!

Listen for:
- attitude — upbeat, confident, intelligent, happy, and pleasant-sounding voices.
- clarity of words.
- clarity of message.
- the kind of voice you would like to hear on the other end of the line if you were calling an office to schedule an appointment or get information.
- the important information — name and best contact phone number.

Listening to all of the entire messages in your inbox can be VERY time consuming and can be delegated to someone else to weed out the really bad ones, so that you only hear the good ones. Once you have done this step a few times, you will be able to quickly determine the good ones from the bad.

Delete the messages of those you would not hire:
- when you cannot understand what they are saying.
- if they ramble on and on.
- if they sound down, uneducated, or unpleasant.
- if they did not leave their phone number or name (even if it shows up in the caller ID system).

Just get those unfavorable messages out of your inbox quickly, so you can focus on the good messages. Do not hesitate or second-guess yourself with this step because you feel desperate to hire someone. The right candidates will show up. Remember, hire slow, and fire fast. If they do not sound exactly like what you are looking for before you hire them, they will never sound like you want after they are hired.

NOTE: Definitely keep the messages of those you do hire, so you have an example to listen to the next time you go through the hiring process.

STEP 6: Set a Date and Time to Conduct a Group Interview in Your Office

Set a date and time that does not conflict with anything you do or a really busy part of your day. Make sure that if you have more than one calendar, the group interview time and date goes on *all* your calendars.

A group interview is another great time-saver. It allows you to be able to see all prequalified candidates face-to-face, at one time. That way, if someone does not look the part (unhealthy, messy, smells like cigarettes, etc.), then you do not waste time with a one-on-one interview for that person(s). A weeknight after business hours typically works best, and the whole group interview process should be about forty-five minutes to an hour. Step 8 describes what to do at the group interview.

STEP 7: Phone Call to Invite to Group Interview

After listening to all the incoming voice messages, deleting the ones you are not interested in, make notes and call back people whose message sounded really good.

The purposes of this step are:
- to give you another opportunity to hear their phone skills. If bad during this call, then do not invite to the interview.
- to find out how far away they live from the job location. If too far, they likely won't show for the interview or work for you very long.
- to find out if they will be able to work the hours required for this position.
- to find out anything you feel needs to be addressed to potentially weed out unqualified candidates. For example, we sometimes will let them know on the phone

that this position requires them to be available for at least one weeknight seminar per week. So, if kids or school or anything else is an obstacle for availability, then we know that person is no longer a candidate, and we move on to the next candidate.

NOTE: They may have called a lot of different companies looking for employment, so you will need to say your name, your company name, the exact name of the position in the ad you placed, and that you are returning their call from the message they left on your voicemail.

You do not want to spend too much time on the phone. This is not meant to be a full phone interview. You are simply feeling this person out for any red flags, and you can make brief notes on your list if need be for these individuals. Unless there is a big red flag for the person during the process thus far, it's better to have these people come to the group interview so that you have the full picture before making the decision.

As long as the brief call goes well, then you can invite them to the scheduled group interview and ask them bring their resume. It is your choice to make them aware that it is a group interview or not. If they ask why it is a group interview, simply tell them that sometimes up to 50% of applicants never show up and you need to be efficient with your time. Make a note on your list if they are a "yes" or "no" to attend the interview.

If you call them and get voicemail, listen for any "red flags" in their outgoing message such as cursing, loud music, or anything inappropriate. When you leave a message, you, of course, are just letting them know who you are and that you are calling to speak with them about the position they inquired about. Leave your best contact number. If they are still looking for a job, they will typically call back promptly.

Contribution from Alex Cantaboni

You've got to ask the question, "How is the drive going to affect you?" There are two girls that, I believe, have left me because it was a long drive to work, and I don't think it's the whole drive to work. It's the drive home. I mean, you're off at 5, and you live forty-five minutes away -- that's a beat down if it takes twice as long because of traffic.

That starts beating them down, especially if they have kids, and they have to feed their family. I approach it more as re-creating the story of, "After a long day, do you mind getting off at 5 and having to drive an hour and half home?" Some people you can get that gut feeling that, yeah, it doesn't bother them driving to and from the shop, and some of them just hate it.

Even if it's a real easy drive, some people can't get around it, so no matter how much they love their day and their job, at the end of the day if it ends negative, it's going to become a negative job and they will leave.

STEP 8: Group Interview

When people start showing up for the interview, it is important to be prepared for the process to go smoothly. Don't be surprised if you invite ten people and only three to four show up. There are a million possible reasons why people don't show up for an interview. Just be with the people who did show up and continue through the process.

If you have current employees who will be working long term with the new hire, it is a good idea to have them observe the candidates as they arrive and during the group interview process. Two sets of eyes are usually better than one, and they may notice things you didn't. People usually respond to the boss differently than toward coworkers, so you need to know how everyone else will be treated.

Pay attention to the candidates as they arrive. You are seeing them for the first time. How did they arrive? Did they have their own vehicle? Did someone else drive them? Did they walk or use public transportation? What do they look like? Are they dressed appropriately? Do they appear to be clean and neat? Are they friendly and interact with the other candidates? Are they early or just on time?

Do not allow anyone into the interview after the start time! Even if they are only one or two minutes late. It will show the other applicants that you will NOT tolerate tardiness. Generally if someone calls to say that they will be late, we thank them and let them know that they have missed their opportunity, as we must start on time.

Items needed for the group interview:

- List of names of candidates who should be attending.
- Know the number of candidates to expect.
- Name tags to be filled out when they arrive.
- Clipboards for each person.
- Questionnaires for each person (see example below).
- Stapler.
- Pens — though the applicants should bring their own pen.
- Notepads and pens for the interviewers.
- The folder with job descriptions and instructions for the interviewers.
- List of things for you to go over after candidates fill out the **first half of the written questionnaire.** For example, more detail on the job description and duties, work hours, when you intend to hire, dress code, pay structure and benefits offered, description of the kind of person who is the best fit and not a fit for this job. For example, you can list the section from the outgoing

message script, "This job is for you if/this job is not for you if . . ."

At the beginning of the interview, before you hand out the questionnaire, tell everyone that you may be hiring more than one person. Ask them to make a note of other applicants they think they would like to work with if they are selected for the position.

Then hand out the questionnaire, which serves several purposes: to find out what their handwriting looks like, whether they listened to instructions, whether they are able to learn something new. You will also see how clearly they are able to communicate — if they cross out answers a lot, make spelling errors, or keep questionnaire materials tidy and answers concise.

While they are filling out the first half of the questionnaire, jot down things that will help you remember who is who, such as the color of their outfit, length of hair, and type of shoes. This will give you a chance to see how much they prepared.

Once they are done filling out the first half of the questionnaire go over the above mentioned job description, pertinent information about your company and take questions. There shouldn't be too many questions at this point, but you want to pay attention to who is asking good questions and how the candidates are interacting with each other.

After you have answered questions, let candidates know that they can now answer the second half of the questionnaire, they can return them to you along with their resume, and they are free to go at that point.

Let them know that you will be calling candidates back within 24 hours to say one of two things:

a) "Thank you so much for attending the interview. I'd like to schedule a one-on-one interview with you if you are still interested in this position."

OR . . .

b) "Thank you so much for attending the interview; however, I cannot offer you the position. I wish you the best of luck in your job search."

Thank them for their time, and the group interview is concluded.

DO NOT HIRE BASED ON WHO IS THE MOST ENTHUSIASTIC OR THE ONE YOU LIKE THE MOST.

Over the many years of hiring employees for our companies, we have tried to take shortcuts. However, we have learned that often the ones we thought would be amazing ended up failing miserably, and the ones who we thought would be just okay ended up being superstars.

There are many factors that go into choosing the right candidate. Be open-minded to each person and go through the whole hiring process.

REMEMBER: **"Hire slow, fire fast!"**

Contribution from Aaron Miller

One of the things that was the oddest to me about the whole hiring process, and probably to most people, is the group interview. It took a while to get used to doing group interviews, but now I have experienced it, it is a really good idea because I can see how [candidates] interact with each other. It's really easy to see a night and day difference between people who are there, particularly because I am always looking for somebody who can talk on the phone *and* be great interacting with people in person. I need somebody who is more outgoing and who can hold a conversation. The group interview definitely helps with figuring that out.

The following is a clear example of the questionnaire to have candidates fill out at the interview. In the example questionnaire please note that the first question is given twice, once in the first half of the questionnaire and then again in the second half. We purposely give them the definition of the term functional medicine after the candidates fill out the first half of the questionnaire while presenting pertinent information about the company. The purpose of having the question twice is to find out who is listening and can learn by auditory information. Most of the instructions you give them in their job will be verbal, so you need to know who is able to receive information just by listening.

You can download this questionnaire and change the questions for your own use by visiting our website www.BBMMUSA.com/p/Hiring .

EXAMPLE QUESTIONNAIRE

Dr. Shwaluk's NTC Health and Fitness

Name:_____Phone:_____

1.   What is functional medicine?

2.   What is the finest quality an employee can offer an employer?

3.   Why do you think some people succeed in life and others fail?

4.   How would you be described by your best friend?

5.   How do you work under pressure?

(Do not answer the following questions at this time)

54

1. What is functional medicine?

2. Are there any circumstances at home or in your personal life that would interfere with your performance at this clinic and with the job as described?

3. How does your lifestyle reflect the health philosophy of this clinic?

4. On average, how many times per year do you get sick (i.e., flu/viruses, headaches, etc.)?

5. Can you work occasional evenings (at least 4 per month)?

6. Do you still want the job?

7. Please give any additional comments, if you desire.

STEP 9: Review Your Notes and Their Resumes

Once all candidates have left the group interview, it is time to review their answers on the group interview questionnaire and your notes. This is also the time to look at their resumes in order to see their employment history and past work experience.

Scan through their questionnaire and resume to see if they at least know how to type, spell, and use correct grammar. It is so wonderful to look at just a few resumes, rather than wasting time muddling through stacks of resumes of people who are not truly interested in working.

Look closely at their resume to see if they are a "job-hopper" or a long-term player.

Choose the best overall candidates to call back for one-on-one interviews. These should be the best of the best from this whole process.

STEP 10: Call to Invite to 1-on-1 Interview

Call candidates back as soon as you can to schedule interviews. We typically call them back that same day (before 8:00 PM) or the next morning. Everyone who attended the group interview should get a phone call within 24 hours of the interview.

These calls should be very quick and easy, and should be:

a) *"Thank you so much for attending the interview, I'd like to schedule a one-on-one interview with you if you are still interested in this position."* Then go ahead and schedule the interview.

OPTIONAL — Let them know that you would like them to email you a brief note of why they want the job and their salary history before the interview. This will let you know if they have good written communication skills and what kind of pay they are used to receiving.

OR, for those you will not hire . . .

b) *"Thank you so much for attending the interview; however, I cannot offer you the position. I wish you the best of luck in your job search."*

The ones with whom you do not offer to do a one-on-one interview commonly already know that they did not get the job, and will say thank you for not leaving them hanging. Rarely will they ever ask why they were not chosen. If they do ask, just say that there were other candidates who were more qualified. Do not say anything more than that.

It may feel awkward to make these calls; however, it is actually quite easy. Just like ripping off a bandage, do it quick and get it over and done with!

STEP 11: 1-on-1 Interview

When they come in for the one-on-one interview, of course, you go over specifics from their resume and ask probing questions about specific duties and expectations to make sure they are the right person.

After one-on-one interviews you should know who your top candidates are, who would be the best fit all around for your business.

Contribution from Alex Cantaboni

In the one-on-one interview I sometimes ask candidates questions about the actual ad, just to see if they even read it, because I have some people that don't. One guy straight up said, "I just saw $12, and I'm here." Clearly only interested in money and not what he would be doing to earn that money.

Some of my first questions are, "What did you understand about the ad? Did you read our reviews or look at our website?" I don't really care, really, what they've done in the past, because we tend to hire people who have a good attitude and don't have experience. People can be trained to follow good systems.

It is important to do interviews every week. Like Jerry says, "Always be hiring." If you look at interviews like you're going to hate them, you will. But I challenge you to look at it as though you're testing yourself to get better at interviews. So, it's like a course for yourself — it will make you a better person. Like, talking in front of people. The more you do it, the better and more natural it becomes. I've noticed that I don't get nervous anymore. I try to make it fun, but I try to hit them hard with the real questions, and I bet you nobody goes through an interview like my interview.

Before I used to ask questions like, "Do you mind working 50 hours a week?" Well, anybody who wants a job is going to say yes to that because they need a job, they need to get paid. Now I ask questions such as: "What are your goals in life? How do you see yourself?" I ask questions that show I care about them, so the questions are about them, yet also understanding that they must fit the right puzzle and fit in with us.

I also ask candidates, "How do you think you can help the team, and how do you think you're going to enjoy your job? What do you see are the positives of pest control?"

Now you know the main steps to our hiring system. Once you have these steps set up the whole hiring process becomes simple and easy. Recently we placed an ad on a Monday afternoon and hired a superstar Tuesday morning. It can happen that simply and easily. The next chapter will make the process even easier.

Chapter 3: Hiring System Part 2

The biggest mistake employers make when hiring is to hire the person who has the most enthusiasm during the interviews. YIKES!

They have jumped through all the hoops to get to this point, yet you have an obligation to your company to do some further due diligence with the possible employees to cover all your legal bases and to make sure you are hiring the right people for your company.

As an employer you legally cannot come right out and ask certain questions, such as those about:

- age
- sex
- marital status
- children
- citizenship
- disability
- housing
- race
- financial status
- a possible criminal record (in some states)

There are also more intangible ways of being that are difficult to assess, such as:

- attitudes toward supervisors, workplace theft, drugs, safety

- opinions
- likelihood of long-term employment
- customer service ability
- ability to learn
- the amount of supervision they require

The following are ways to determine this information AND to set GROUND RULES for working at your business.

There is no particular order to these items.

A) "Try Before You Buy"

After the one-on-one interview you can then invite the candidates to try the position for a half or full day. Tell them that you will pay them for their time and negotiate the appropriate pay rate.

We do the "try it for a day" for three main reasons:

a) This gives *them* the opportunity to find out what the work environment is like and the details of the job.

b) This gives *you* the opportunity to find out if they are a fit in your company culture and are able to do the job.

c) When you invite them to try it for a day, let them know that if all works out they will be going for a background check and drug test. Don't be surprised if they don't show up. This saves you a lot of time in unnecessary training.

If, by the end of the day they are still interested in the position, and you are still interested in them, this may be a great fit for your team!

During the "try it before you buy it" trial period, pay attention to your team and get their input on the quality of the candidate.

I had a conversation with a candidate in my chiropractic office one time. . . . It was a "try working here for a week to see how it goes" scenario. During the group and one-on-one interviews she did well, but not great. So, I wasn't 100% sure one way or the other. By the time we got to Wednesday, after having a conversation with my team, I pulled her into my office and I said, "I don't think that this is working out."

She asked, "Why?"

I said, "Because it occurs to me you're doing just enough to not get fired, and that's unacceptable. I am here to do a job that is exceptional for our patients, and I need superstars to help back me up. So, if you can't do this job as a superstar, then please take your things."

As she did, she said, "No one's ever said it to me like that before, and I appreciate you being straightforward."

I said, "Okay. Thank you." And I made sure that she got her paycheck right then and there for the hours that she worked.

B) Opinion Survey: Find Out Their Attitudes

An opinion survey helps assess the more intangible ways of being and attitude that are difficult to assess in an interview.

We use the "Orion 1" assessment by The Nielson Group. It is a simple online questionnaire that takes about twenty minutes to complete right at your business. If you fill out the form at www.BBMMUSA.com/p/Hiring you will receive an email with the link to The Neilson Group.

Additionally, this survey lets you know if a person is likely to lie or tell the truth. This assessment is NOT bulletproof for gauging honesty; however, it can save you a lot of angst.

If it says, **"Based on company guidelines, this applicant may be considered further for employment,"** they are likely telling the truth with their answers.

If it says, **"The subject may be attempting to alter the results of the survey. Based on company guidelines, this applicant may not be considered further for employment,"** thank them for coming in and tell them you cannot offer them the position.

DO NOT hire them if it says, **"This applicant may not be considered further for employment,"** no matter how much you like them!!!!!

Contribution by Alex Cantaboni

The Orion test helps a lot. It's weird, like a second gut feeling. I would say it works more accurately with the girls in the office than it does the guys. We were having some struggles with one girl, and the survey told us we would have those issues. Not enough to not have her work for us, but enough to make us rethink that maybe she should be doing something else in the company rather than her current position.

She's amazing at answering phones. Smile, happiness, and all that stuff, but scheduling is just not her thing.

The Orion test told us she would be good; we just had to put her in the right position.

C) Background Check and Drug Test

The companies we use in the Plano/Richardson area are called FC Background and Fastest Labs of Plano.

They have a variety of tests for drugs, the background check, and FC Background also has a test that assesses the applicant's ability to learn and the amount of supervision they'll require.

Contribution from Aaron Miller

The Orion is a great survey; it really helps out a lot, kind of like figuring out where they are and what they're thinking. But the background check was crazy to me, or at least the drug screening. I had a lady who was a professional and interviewed great, said all the right things. I didn't offer the job but I said, "This is great. The next step is, here's the drug screening, and you've got . . . " whatever it was — half an hour to get there or something like that.

Well, it took her, like, two hours, and when I got the results back, she still failed. It just blew me away. I wouldn't have expected that. . . . Definitely [do] the background check. I haven't had anything pull up on anybody on that, but it's always a good idea, particularly when you're dealing with sensitive information like we do. To make sure that you've dotted all your i's and crossed all your t's. At least as best as you can.

Let's see. . . . Then we had the guy that was dealing drugs out of our ice cream store. That was awesome. Yeah.

We had three eventually drug dealers. This one time, I picked up the phone, and this guy on the phone says, "The gate is open."

"The gate, it's open. I have no idea what you're talking about."
"Sorry, wrong number." He hangs up and I mention this to one
of the kids that are working there. "Oh, yeah! That was for this
guy. He was selling drugs out of the store." "Oh, well thank you
for telling me now." He was also a graffiti artist. Who knew?

D) New Employee Forms

These are legal documents that you are required to have every
new hire fill out and that you must keep for at least a year. It
may be longer in some states.

a) Employment Application: NEVER write on someone's
application. This could be used in a court of law, so
comments, impressions, or any other notations may
count against you. Always have the applicant fill out the
form in your establishment so that they don't take it
home and have someone else fill it out for them with
inaccurate information.

b) Form I-9, Employment Eligibility Verification: This
ensures that the person you are hiring is legal to work in
this country.

c) Form W-4, Employee's Withholding Allowance
Certificate: This form is used in calculating the correct
federal income tax withheld from the employee's pay.
Consider having a new Form W-4 filled out each year
and when the employee's personal or financial situation
changes (e.g., divorce, number of children, etc.).

d) Emergency contact information: Make a copy of this
information and keep it handy in an easily accessible
place in case of urgent need, rather than locked up in the
employee file.

E) Employee Policies

Every company is run differently, and employees have different levels of experience in being a good employee. The best way to avoid conflict or disappointment in your employees is to have VERY CLEAR guidelines of your expectations of them. Each employee's job must have clearly written standard operating procedures. This is what ensures that they do their job to expectations.

In addition to the procedures manuals, your company must also have a clearly written policy manual. The policy manual describes the rules of conduct of the business and applies to every employee in the business. Clear expectations are especially vital with people who are new to the workforce or who have been out of the workforce for a while. If someone has not had many jobs, they may not know that they must play by rules of conduct in order to keep their job.

The policy manual is a document that employees read and sign. You then give them a copy of the signed document to take home for their records.

You need to be really clear with every employee on exactly what you will and won't tolerate in your business as well as on the level of performance or standards you expect from your employees. The following is a guideline of the essentials that must be in your policy manual. The following outline is available as a download for free by filling out the easy form at www.BBMMUSA.com/p/Hiring

Employee Policy Manual Essentials

1. Introduction
- nature of employment (For example, Texas is a right-to-work state, meaning employees have a right to work, not a right to be part of a union.)

- business's compliance with laws, e.g., ASA
- anti-harassment policy

2. Benefits
- vacation, sick days, jury duty, workers' compensation, holidays, health insurance, leaves of absence, military leave, and employee purchases
- who qualifies for benefits and when benefits start

3. Communication Standards
 How will the company communicate with employees: text? call? email?

4. Employee Pay
- commission, overtime, pay period, time of day paychecks are distributed
- process of check distribution

5. Introductory/Probationary Period
Outline what the time is meant for and how long it will last — e.g., 90 days.

6. Categories of Employment
- part time, full time, temporary, number of hours per week
- time-keeping processes

7. Basic Business Information
- hours of operation, work vehicle policy

8. Employee Breaks
- length of time, thirty minutes of unpaid lunch- statement that a break is not mandatory or required within 9 hours (Check with the laws in your state!)

9. Employee Work Expectations (for each employee)
- absence, tardiness, smoking, parking, cleanliness, appearance, dress code, work hours, **telephone and social media** usage (In Texas, at the time of writing this book, employers are allowed to

have employees put their personal cell phone in a locker while at work so as not to be interrupted.)

10. Work Place Violence
- what is considered violent behavior
- threats, documentation

11. Background Checks
- calls to past employers: dates given, termination, position, rehire?

12. Technology Resources
- appropriate use of company "staff" phone, voicemail, computers, printers, software, email, internet

13. Definition of Theft
- time, objects, money

14. Proper Care for Any and All Equipment
- proper maintenance

15. Training
- any and all training
- costs: who pays
- paid or unpaid training

16. Drug & Alcohol Policy
- circumstances in which screening is required and the location of screening

17. Corrective Action of the Above Guidelines
-All of the standards, expectations, and guidelines must be enforced with each employee or you cannot use the policy at all.

18. Employee Acknowledgement Form
- signature page

A Conversation between Jerry Kezhaya and Danielle Hasting

Jerry: Actually, it was a Sunday morning at 6:00 AM when I drove by my building. *Sunday morning at 6:00 AM.* That means all night Saturday night a door to my building was propped open. It wasn't like it was just left ajar — those doors automatically close because they are designed to close. So I called my manager at six o'clock Sunday morning and said: "Hello, you need to get to the building right now. You have a problem!" If they are the manager, then they are responsible. The door propped open overnight has not happened since that phone call.

Danielle: That's one of the things that I put in our policy manual too, because our back door doesn't close all the way, all the time. It must be checked, especially at the end of the day. The last person out the door is the one responsible for making sure the door is closed properly and locked. If you weren't the last person and it's ajar, let the person before you know, "Hey, you didn't shut it all the way," so they're aware of it for the next time they exit that door. If you're the last one out, and I come in and find the door open, that's an automatic write-up.

I explain it to them by saying, "Listen, I'm not trying to be a dick about it. I'm worried about your safety and mine. If that door is left open, anybody can come in. And you know what? No one would know if something bad happened."

If everybody else leaves, and I hear somebody walking around in the back, I know that should be somebody who works here because there should be no one coming through the back door unless they have a key.

Jerry: Well, you just have to hold your people accountable. That's the big issue you have, right? It sounds to me like there may be some leniency there.

Danielle: Should I write them up the first time or give them a verbal warning?

Jerry: You have to write them up. You need to be serious. If you're going to let them slide on this one, you have to let them slide on the next one too. I encourage you to make holding them accountable a habit before it becomes too difficult to enforce.

F) Employee Training

When an employee starts their job, it is imperative that they get up to speed as quickly as possible. You do not want to waste time or money in lengthy training. About a week of training is usually sufficient.

The best ways to train new employees are a combination of:
a) Really well-written and easy to read Standard Operating Procedures (SOP's). (See the Systems Module on our website www.BBMMUSA.com for how to create SOPs quickly and effectively. It may be the topic of our next book.) SOPs must include everything the employee is expected to do, from opening to closing of their shift. Commonly it is a checklist of items and clear instructions on how to complete each task.
b) Hands-on working with someone to see how the job is done and then switching roles to do the job while being coached on the details. It may or may not be best to have the person leaving the position teaching the new hire. Consider that if a lot of procedures have changed recently or if the person leaving is not following the SOPs, then they may not be the best person to train the new hire.

c) Staff meetings where you role play and talk about different scenarios in their jobs.

Contribution by Aaron Miller

Make sure you've got your SOPs in place to make it easy to train new employees. This means that you have all your procedures and policies written down in a step-by-step order so that they learn what they need to be doing as quickly as possible. Creating videos on different parts of the process or writing out checklists can also be very helpful in making sure that they can get up to speed as quickly as possible. So, spending some time to make sure that you have those procedures written down is extremely important.

If you don't have your SOPs documented and organized, then their job is to write down what you teach them so that, if you have to replace them, at least you have a starting point for the next person. This way the next person can stand on the shoulders of the person in front of them.

I have found that if I don't have a procedure written out, I usually end up doing the job myself or they do it their way or not at all. It costs me more time and defeats the purpose of having the employee.

G) Employee Retention

When your company is a great business to work for, people will seek you out.

Why do employees quit? *They do NOT feel appreciated by their direct supervisor.*

Why Do Good Employees Leave?

Excerpt by David W. Richard

A study came up with the surprising finding: If you're losing good people, look to their immediate supervisors. More than any other single reason, he is the reason people stay and thrive in [an] organization. And he's the reason why they quit, taking their knowledge, experience and contacts with them. Often, straight to the competition.

"People leave managers, not companies," write the authors Marcus Buckingham and Curt Coffman. "So much money has been thrown at the challenges of keeping good people — in the form of better pay, better perks and better training — when in the end, turnover is mostly a manager issue."

If you have a turnover problem, look first to your managers and supervisors.

Beyond a point, an employee's primary need has less to do with money, and more to do with how he's treated and how valued he feels. Much depends directly on the immediate manager.

Five Top Reasons Employees Love Their Jobs
1. *Coworkers*
2. *Organizational culture*
3. *Autonomy*
4. *Variety/Learning*
5. *Being challenged*

Employee happiness is contagious. This in turn engages and motivates employees to be their best, most positive selves.

Contribution by Alex Cantaboni

To me, it's both. An employee needs a good attitude *and* workmanship. Every time I have an employee with a bad

71

attitude, even if they're the best worker I've ever had, the rest of the team will be brought down further and further by them.

I'm starting to learn in life that the mind is very powerful. It's more powerful than anything we've got. More powerful than the heart. More powerful than the body. If someone has a negative attitude in the company, it will impact the company in a negative way. For example, the other employees will start thinking the same negative thoughts, especially if they are very vocal with their negativity. So, quickly getting rid of people with a negative attitude is very important.

When the people are happy, you will have longer retention and more good workers.

By the time you get to this point you will have superstar employees hired and well on their way to being trained to follow the systems you have set up.

Congratulations!

We hope these people work out great for you for a very long time. However, the following chapter is what to do if things don't work out, and they must be fired. Just like having a system for hiring, you must have a system for firing, so set it up now, before you are in a firing situation.

Chapter 4: Effective Firing

There are a multitude of books and manuals on how to effectively fire an employee and how to keep out of trouble with legal problems or the government when firing an employee.

The main thing to keep in mind is that you MUST tell the employee what the rules are to begin with!!!!

In your company's Employee Policy Manual you have made it clear what actions are grounds for immediate dismissal and the rules they must abide by. If your employees have not read and signed the Employee Policy Manual, then you might not have any ground to stand on.

When it comes time to terminate someone's employment, one of the most helpful tools to fire legally, while informing the employee of the infractions they are making, is the four-step process of the "Corrective Discipline Counseling System" by Star Business Forms. An exact example of what this form looks like follows this section. It is fairly self-explanatory. The four-step process form helps you fire them in a systematic way, so as to cut down on your likelihood of lawsuits or increases in pay rate to state unemployment.

If an employee is really bringing morale down in the office, not doing their job or being disruptive to the business, then it may be worth it to skip the four-step process of the Corrective Discipline Counseling System because it will be worth it to pay the increase in unemployment insurance just to get them out of your company.

Basically the four-step process of the Corrective Discipline Counseling System is a written document of the communication you and the employee have had regarding the policies that have been broken.

The Corrective Discipline Counseling form is a carbon copy form that has four layers on top of each other. The first layer is the first write-up and is considered a verbal warning of the policy that has been broken. It includes the employee name and date.

If the employee understands and agrees, they sign the form. If they don't agree, there is a short space for them to write a rebuttal and then sign the form. The top piece is theirs to keep, reminding them of the infraction.

The next time a policy is broken, you use the same form you started with for that employee, only you use the second layer down. The second and third write-ups are NOT verbal warnings. Make it clear to the employee that the forth write-up is when they are fired.

There does not have to be four write-ups on the same policy, such as "They left the door open." No, it can be any problem with an employee, particularly disregard for the written policies. You may write up an employee for getting to work late, playing computer games on company time, being out of uniform, or any other policy in your company policy manual.

When you start writing up people seriously and regularly, your employees will know that you take your policies seriously and they must follow the rules or their employment with you will be terminated.

The more you practice holding your employees accountable, the easier it'll become for you. It'll become second nature. And the employee says, "Holy crap! Wow! That guy's not joking."

They are right. We are not joking. We have a business to run, are not here to play or put up with drama. If they want to play around and break the rules, they can go home. We're here to get stuff done.

Sometimes, somewhere inside ourselves, we think that we have to get permission to write up and hold employees accountable. I'm telling you right now, you have permission because it is your company.

If you find it difficult to have disciplinary conversations, then we recommend that you write down what you need to say in point form, then role play with someone to practice what you are going to say and possible responses from the employee. Rehearsing the conversation allows you to have the conversation point-blank. The first time can be a little shaky.

The conversation can simply follow something like this: "Come here. We need to talk. This is what I saw happen ____ (fill in the blank)____ . Tell me about it." And they tell you, and then you say, "Okay. Well, this is what *needed* to happen. Is this something that you still feel that you could actually do? 'Cause if you can't do it anymore, then we may need to go our separate ways."

Note: Record the conversation. If the workforce commission interviews you the transcript of the recording can be submitted as evidence that you counseled the employee on proper policies and procedures.

FORM CODE: 1215
REORDER FROM: STAR BUSINESS FORMS / HUNT HENSON (800) 888-7199

VISIT US AT http://www.starform.com

CORRECTIVE DISCIPLINE
COUNSELING SYSTEM
This process can be accelerated if the nature of the incident requires it.

Employee Name/Number _____

VERBAL COUNSELING VERIFICATION

Reference to Personnel Rule/Regulation	Date of Incident

SUMMARY

RESPONSE

Did Employee Accept?

Employee Signature   Date   Supervisor Signature

WRITTEN WARNING RECORD

Reference to Personnel Rule/Regulation	Date of Incident

SUMMARY

RESPONSE

Did Employee Accept?

Employee Signature   Date   Supervisor Signature

SECOND WRITTEN WARNING or WORK SUSPENSION NOTICE
(From ___ / ___ / ___   Thru ___ / ___ / ___)

Reference to Personnel Rule/Regulation	Date of Incident

SUMMARY

RESPONSE

Did Employee Accept?

Employee Signature   Date   Supervisor Signature

EMPLOYEE TERMINATION RECORD

Reference to Personnel Rule/Regulation	Date of Incident

SUMMARY

RESPONSE

Did Employee Accept?

Employee Signature   Date   Supervisor Signature

76

Be Cutthroat

Contribution by Alex Cantaboni

Employees are replaceable. So, if you get that feeling like someone's not doing their job, don't feel bad; just get rid of them and move to the next person. Like Jerry says, "always be hiring" because there's someone out there who might be the perfect candidate that you never gave the opportunity because you didn't create the space for them.

We set expectations high, to train them in the habits we like to see in the company. For example, "If you're late in the next 90 days, you're gone. No ifs, ands, or buts. No excuses."

You have to have processes and procedures in place to fire people. Unfortunately, the state doesn't want you to just let them go without lot's of paperwork. Following up with the employee and making sure that you have documented warning notices set in place, and making sure that you are letting that employee know that you know something's going on, and following up with that are essential.

The write-up steps are making them aware of it, keeping track on paper, and letting them have their response to it so that if it continues happening and then you let them go, you have the necessary paperwork.

I'm really good at putting pressure on people. I guess some people call it micromanaging. When my employees start getting micromanaged by me, it's because there's something they're not doing right, so I kind of hound them about it, and I nitpick it and just see if they can go above and beyond it, survive, and improve. But I would say 75% of employees give up and don't want to deal with their mess anymore.

We had a guy that we pushed out because he was being negative. We even brought it up with him and said, "Hey, listen, you're being really negative. Stop that."

We had that conversation with him multiple times because he was never negative with me, but always negative with the guys and the management team. He was very good at hiding it from me. Here's where it can be really hard. You have to open your ears and listen to your staff. You have to make them comfortable with telling you things because, if not, you might never know what's really going on.

Over time it seems like if you just probe and ask the right questions, bad employees just kind of break down. I had an employee who left us on his own terms, but leaving because of all the questions I asked him over the previous six months. The questions made him start thinking that I'm aware of the things that he's doing and I'm not stupid. Down to the point where one day he was frustrated, and I was, like, "All right. Tell me what you think I owe you. Tell me what pay rate that you think you deserve and how much you're worth to me," and he came in and it was some stupid and ridiculous amount that he didn't even sit down and think about.

I countered his offer with something that I thought was acceptable. I'm sure that didn't help him, and I knew he wouldn't be employed here for very much longer because that's what he really thought he deserved.

Don't ignore problem employees. Don't sweep things under the rug. If you do, eventually it's going to affect your business. He's already moved on to another job. It probably didn't even harm him at all, but now look at all the challenges I have to go through to find or replace him.

Now, regarding your employees' personal appearance — especially the technicians who might not be very interested in their personal appearance — how do you get them to straighten up? Like, tuck in their shirt, shave, all that stuff?

That's the ruthless part. They just have to do it.

[In] one of my first jobs when I was younger, they were going to send me home on my first day because I didn't come in shaven. Luckily, I had a good manager, and he said, "You know, let's just finish the route. " At the end of the day, Just promise me you'll shave in the morning."

I think you need to be very ruthless and tell them, "This is the way. This is what I'm trying to create. If not, there's the door." When people are being held accountable, we see the changes in simple things, like tucking a shirt in.

I explain the reason why policies and procedures are important too. For example, I said, "People are judgmental. They see that you walk in with your shirt untucked. They see that you didn't shave. They see that you just woke up and don't really care about your life or your day. Clients don't want someone like that in their home. " Sometimes employees just need some guidance.

I try to give them an example. Like, "When you drive up, and there's another pest control guy with shorts on and a ripped T-shirt, don't you think that sets a bad example for the other company?" At some point, you have to be cutthroat. You have to hold them to your standards. That's part of the company policy. It's in the policy book. Shave. Tuck your shirt in.

I think it's sad, but it's getting easier to fire people. It's the same as hiring; it's repetition. In the beginning, I just got discouraged. I wondered if I would ever get the right employees. Now, it's still sad that we have to go through this, but you just see the evolution of your staff. It really sucks to go through firing people, but there's always someone better.

Sexual Harassment

Let me tell you a story about a bookkeeper. She wasn't doing her job. She was slacking off, showing up late, not paying bills or taxes on time, and costing me a lot of money in late fees. So, we went through the four-part process of writing her up and firing her. Interestingly she agreed that the job was over her head, and she recommended her friend to come work for us. About three weeks later we got a letter in the mail from the Texas Workforce Commission indicating that she was filing for unemployment insurance on the basis of sexual assault.

WHAT??? What a shock!!! Like a punch out of nowhere.

Normally there wouldn't be a section on sexual harassment in a book about hiring; however, we want you to be prepared for accusations that may not be true. That is why this section is in the chapter about firing. The thing is that even though we knew the accusation wasn't true, it still sent us for a loop and made me question if there was anything I ever said or did that might be construed as sexual harassment.

Of course there wasn't anything I could think of that would be considered harassment, and the state agreed with me, as they denied the claim for unemployment payments to the employee. The main reason the claim was denied was because of the thoroughness of our documentation system for corrective action. DOCUMENTATION is the single greatest tool you have on your side when it comes to a "she said/ he said" situation. It is important to save all emails, text messages, and written notes, just in case you need them as proof of innocence at a later date. Saving the email where the bookkeeper suggested her friend come to work for us instead of her was one of the helpful pieces of evidence, as no one being harassed would suggest their friend work at the same place.

It is difficult to protect yourself 100% of the time because it is your word against the word of another person. The only way to truly protect yourself is to have a third person or more in the room at all times when with an employee. This is difficult to do, so you must make sure your documentation is really good.

Hopefully you will never be in this situation; however, if you ever are accused of sexual harassment and it isn't true, you'll have your documentation to back you up.

Workplace Harassment Is a Form of Discrimination

Harassment is a form of discrimination that violates Title VII of the Civil Rights Act of 1964 and other federal authority in the United States of America.

When we looked at the Federal Communications Commission guidelines at https://www.fcc.gov/encyclopedia/understanding-workplace-harassment-fcc-staff, we found excellent information on what is and what *isn't* harassment. We also found out that any employee wishing to initiate a complaint arising out of the alleged incident of harassment must contact an FCC Counselor within forty-five calendar days of the date of the incident. At a minimum they must have complained about the incident to a supervisor at the company who got a written statement from both parties about the incident and that must be kept in the employee records.

Hostile work environment harassment occurs when unwelcome comments or conduct based on sex, race, or other legally protected characteristics unreasonably interferes with an employee's work performance or creates an intimidating, hostile, or offensive work environment. Anyone in the workplace might commit this type of harassment — a management official, coworker, or nonemployee, such as a contractor, vendor or guest. The victim can be anyone affected by the conduct, not just the individual at whom the offensive conduct is directed.

Examples of actions that may create sexual hostile environment harassment include:

- Leering, i.e., staring in a sexually suggestive manner
- Making offensive remarks about looks, clothing, body parts
- Touching in a way that may make an employee feel uncomfortable, such as patting, pinching, or intentional brushing against another's body
- Telling sexual or lewd jokes, hanging sexual posters, making sexual gestures, etc.
- Sending, forwarding, or soliciting sexually suggestive letters, notes, emails, or images

Other actions which may result in hostile environment harassment, but are nonsexual in nature, include:

- Use of racially derogatory words, phrases, epithets
- Demonstrations of a racial or ethnic nature, such as a use of gestures, pictures, or drawings that would offend a particular racial or ethnic group
- Comments about an individual's skin color or other racial/ethnic characteristics
- Making disparaging remarks about an individual's gender that are not sexual in nature
- Negative comments about an employee's religious beliefs (or lack of religious beliefs)
- Expressing negative stereotypes regarding an employee's birthplace or ancestry
- Negative comments regarding an employee's age when referring to employees 40 and over
- Derogatory or intimidating references to an employee's mental or physical impairment

What Is Not Harassment?

The antidiscrimination statutes are not a general civility code. Thus, federal law does not prohibit simple teasing, offhand comments, or isolated incidents that are not extremely serious. Rather, the conduct must be so objectively offensive as to alter

82

the conditions of the individual's employment. The conditions of employment are altered only if the harassment culminates in a tangible employment action or is sufficiently severe or pervasive to create a hostile work environment.

Even though harassment does not necessarily include simple off-color jokes or comments that cause someone to feel offended, we recommend that you don't even talk about sex, tell off jokes, or make any comments of a sexual or offensive nature in any way, shape, or form while at work OR around any of your employees. Period.

Do *Not* Hire Friends or Family

Contribution from Alex Cantaboni

There are several reasons why I do NOT recommend hiring friends or family. The biggest thing about hiring friends and family is usually either one or both can't separate personal life [from] business life. When I tell them to do something, every reaction of family and friends has been that they talk back to me, and they tell me how they feel about what I want them to do. In business, you should be able to tell someone to do their job and not have them talk back with personal feelings.

With my friend Nick a conversation could start off personal, and then when it turned into business, I told him, "I'm your boss. I'm talking to you as your boss now. I'm telling you what to do." Then because we were friends, sometimes he'd just say, "No," and argue and fight. An employee wouldn't do that, or if they did, then I could always say: "There's the door."

That was the hardest part. We could have a conversation in the morning about some personal stuff, about his girlfriend, my wife, that kind of stuff, and then at 4 o'clock when business came up, "Hey, can you do this and this and this?" He'd always

83

be, like, "Well, why are we doing that? Why are we doing this? Why are we doing it this way?"

So, the hardest thing to do is separate work life from home life. I think it can be done. It's just really hard for me. I'm not saying there aren't family and friends in business that get along. It's just difficult.

The second reason to not hire friends or family is basically they don't think they have the accountability as much as nonrelated employees do. A good example is actually something that happened today: We take the toll tag charges (if they use a company truck for personal reasons) out of their check. For example, to and from work is "personal" because technically they would be driving their vehicle, so once a month we calculate the charges and take that amount out of their paychecks.

It was forgotten during last month's payroll, so we told everyone that we would have this family/friend bookkeeper take it out on the following paycheck, and then it was forgotten about again in today's payroll.

A nonrelated employee would say, "Sorry. I'll get right on it and fix it." In this case, on the second mistake, an employee would have been written up. It is harder for me to hold family and friends accountable because issues at work can create issues at home.

With friends and family, they just move on and think they have their job forever with no repercussions. To them it might just be a job, and they don't have to worry about really representing you and your company. Family and friends — they make excuses for themselves and don't move forward. They don't respect you like regular employees do. There can be huge issues created because you want to maintain a good relationship AND you want them to do the job that you are paying them to do. It takes a special relationship to make it work long term.

Another reason to not hire friends or family is that the passion for the business is commonly different. You also might expect a friend or family member to be there with you if you are working through the night, but you can't expect that of them because it is not their business. I think partnership and hiring only works if both people are supporting each other's weight. You know, they're better at one thing than you are, and you balance each other out.

Additionally, for me, hiring friends was not good. When I took time off, they hated that. They hated that I had time off. I bought a new car, they resented my new car. They made judgments about me because they knew my entire personal situation. They knew that my wife makes decent money. I make good money. They see all of this stuff coming in, so their judgment is huge. When your "friend" sees your house and what you do for fun and what you spend money on, there is a little resentment or jealousy, compared to an employee that doesn't know where I live.

Ethics and sense of urgency to grow the business are other reasons to not hire friends or family. I used to fight a lot with Nick. For example, if somebody called in for service, I wanted to send an available tech right over or even go myself. I'd have it taken care of the same day or the next morning. He just thought it was okay for them to wait, and I think that's true if you don't want to grow as big, fast, and strong as I did. It boiled down to different levels of urgency to get things done. I think a big failure in business is having different types of urgency within the management of the company. . . .

An employee that respects you, even if their urgency isn't like yours . . . you can make them have the urgency like yours because you create that as that's part of their job. Compared to family and friends, the urgency might not be as easy because they probably don't think there's as much of a repercussion. They don't think they will get fired.

Firing Nick was the hardest thing that I've ever had to do, and I think it was only because he was a friend.

We met a little bit before high school. We were in the same church and then high school together. Then out of a desperate situation I said, "Hey, do you need a job? You want to come help me build this business?" That's just where my mind went, and at the time it was good, but now that I look back, all his issues were the same as in the beginning.

It's just that in the beginning, I didn't know what I was doing. For example, I would sometimes offer him 100% of the entire job to go help a client that was panicked and needed service on a Saturday or a Sunday. I mean, one hundred bucks for an hour's worth of work, and the guy would say "No" or bitch and complain, or gripe back at me because I was his friend. Now I look back at those early signs of the differences between us. If I could go back, I know now, that he wouldn't have been the person hired.

It's kind of like going back to the "civilian" thing because not only was I paying him the full amount that the client was paying my company, but I supplied the truck, the chemicals, all that stuff, so I lost money on those deals just to make the client happy. "Civilians" [people who do not have their own business] and employees don't see the cost of doing business.

They have the mindset of an employee, "That I don't have to go do that stuff, and I don't have to respect your truck. I don't see the taxes you pay or the price you pay to be in business." Still to this day he probably thinks everything that I make goes 100% in my pocket. No one really understands until they start their own business how much money really goes out.

What really made everything explode with my friend Nick was when he started affecting all my staff. Over six years of us being friends and working together I got used to his negative attitude and tolerated his way of being. My mind just didn't care. It really was just his "normal" everyday stuff that I learned to tolerate.

Just a normal everyday thing, but when it started affecting the other employees, because he started talking to them and treating them like he was talking to and treating me, I told him, "You can't talk to them that way." I said, "They don't know you. They haven't built an immune system to you like I have," and I said, "Honestly, anything you say, I don't really care anymore because I've learned to just dismiss you. I've learned that you just need to get it out and off your chest, and I'm willing to listen." That's how he needed it to be, very "one-sided."

I said, "But the girls in the office don't understand that, and honestly, the guys don't either. It took me six years of listening to you every day to get used to this, and they are never going to do that." Then, I said, "And the girls in the office, in general, are always more sensitive." So, it started going downhill from there because he started talking bad about me to the staff.

Afterwards, I learned that, literally, what he would tell them about me, but he was him speaking about himself, which seems like the weirdest thing.

For example, I walked back into the office one day because I forgot something, and he was on speaker with Christy, and he was the one actually panicking because I was going out of town.

He was telling her, "Alex is just panicking, and he has all this pressure." He would enhance that, and when I walked in, and I caught him, and I confronted him . . . he tried to reverse it on me. So, I was kind of semi-brainwashed by him. For as strong mentally as I am, I was brainwashed.

One day Nick called the shop and Brandon answered. Nick, thinking it was me, started talking bad about Brandon. Nick thought I was just messing with him because every once in a while I joked with him by making up some weird voices. He thought I was joking at that time, and he said, "Oh, stop messing with me!" He just went on this long ramble about Brandon, never realizing that he was talking with Brandon! He called the guy he was talking bad about, and kept going on and on and on.

I got a phone call at 7:30 that night from Brandon while I was at a networking event. Brandon was really upset! "Alex, Nick said this, this, and this, and I'm done." He said, "I'm not coming into work tomorrow. I quit. I can't work for someone that says all of that about me."

I saved him by saying, "Let's talk about it," and we came up with a game plan for Brandon to replace Nick right then and there. Basically that's when it all came to a head. I trusted my gut feeling that it was time to let Nick go.

I called Nick and said, "Let's meet later." He's like, "What's up?" I said, "Oh, let's just meet at the shop. I've got a few things I want to go over with you. When can you do it?"

We met the next morning at about 10:30, and I simply said, "I love you. I appreciate you helping me, and taking care of my company, but I think it's time to go our separate ways. I don't think you're happy here, and I'm not happy. I wish you the best of luck."

I had a long script in my head, and then I just kind of eliminated it down to one sentence that was pretty simple. I think he already knew it was coming.

Because of our relationship, I knew that it could have become a battle and something that I really didn't want to go through, so, I offered him a separation bonus. I met with Jerry Kezhaya earlier, and we came up with a nice, short document explaining that we are mutually separating and in consideration of receiving the bonus check that he would not file for unemployment against us.

Being prepared helped a lot. It was still very hard.

I had it all written down, and him signing the paperwork was the only way he was going to get that separation bonus. It was enough money to cover a month's pay, which helped a lot. To this day I think it was worth it to provide the bonus because it showed I cared about him, and the outcome was the best we could have had in those circumstances.

His initial reaction when I said to him, "It's time for us to go our separate ways" was: "Oh, I kind of knew that." That's really all he said.

I was actually very happy because, with his initial reaction, it was almost a relief that he saw the separation coming. It became easy to say, "It's just time. You know it," and I just kept saying that, "It's just time." Just kept saying that because he then started trying to pick a fight and get me to have a reaction.

I think one of the last things he said was, "I knew it because it's weird that you wanted me to meet you here." Then I watched him as he packed up his personal things. I treated him just like an employee (not a friend) that was just terminated. I watched him to make sure he wasn't stealing anything. Sometimes that happens because they're frustrated or whatever. I went online and ordered a ride for him and said, "See you later." I wasn't going to give him a ride home anymore. Then after that we just don't really talk.

Jerry Kezhaya and the Business Builders Mastermind helped me through the most difficult situation of my business, because even with our gut feelings, even if we know it, sometimes we still need to find someone to motivate us, lift us up, and push us to do things that help us to move toward our goals. It's not easy to fire a friend. I think it would have been hard if Nick had been just an employee, but it was even that much harder because he was a long-time friend and like family.

Now that I have Brandon as our new manager, I see the huge, huge potential of everything that we've missed over the last six years and where the company could really be if I'd had someone like Brandon working with me back then.

That's why I ask, "Why even put yourself through that? Why even go to friends and family? Why even think about them?" There are so many good people out there that are not associated with you that can help you with your business.

Even if friends or family are desperate, don't hire them. Just tell them up front that you will not hire friends or family. It is okay to say, "I want us to be friends. I want to still be able to go out with you this weekend and not have business cause a strain in our relationship." If you say that, it's easier because then they don't get their feelings hurt and you don't have the guilt. Now, all of my friends know that I don't hire friends or family.

My friendship with Nick has not resumed. He had changed his cell number and did not give it to me, so, when we split ways, I just told him, "Whenever you're ready, I'm here for you." I know I can get his number, but I threw it back at him. It has to be his choice at this point to contact me if he wants to resume our friendship. Nick and my brother are still friends, and when I talked to my brother about it, he agrees that it's probably the best thing that's happened to me, and it's probably the best thing that's happened to Nick too. We didn't match anymore. We just didn't mesh — we no longer had the same goals or wanted the same things.

I would say it is because I grew and he didn't. He also did not see that my goal was actually to have him be a part of this business in a much bigger way and get bigger rewards. It would have happened if he would have been patient enough. He didn't realize that my whole plan and goal was to bring him with me, but he really thought I was just doing all this for myself and not for him too. The business was just changing faster for me, and I was growing faster than he wanted to or was able to grow.

Now, I'm understanding that if Nick would have helped just one more client on Friday, did one extra job a week, did one extra thing for me a week . . . like Brandon's been doing . . . Nick would have gotten a raise. Brandon's already received a substantial pay raise in four months because he's doing all the extra things and is growing in leaps and bounds. He comes to me with what he is working on. I don't have to tell him what to do. Brandon is, like: "Hey, I created an employee handbook. I created this. Hey, I did this." So, it is so much better now, and I didn't have to get after him to do it!

That's also why I know for sure. I feel no regrets and I feel no hard feelings that this all came about. I know 110% the only reason why Nick was where he was at was because of Nick, not because of me. If he would have done the things that the other employees were doing around me, he'd still be with us. I've never once looked back and thought, "Well, maybe you should have done something a little different, Alex. Maybe you should have paid him a little bit more?" But then my wife says that no matter what I would have given him, he never would have been happy, and the other employees see this too. I know I made the right decision.

They have seen that I'm happier. I'm a happier person now and not as stressed, because at the end of the day I don't have a phone call that's going to bring me down. Imagine ending your day every day with a negative phone call.

I had a sense of relief when I told Nick it was time to part ways and he was gone from my business. All the weight on my shoulders became a different type of stress because I had to physically work harder at the time. However, mentally it was easier.

I think that mental stress is more powerful and draining than physical stress. Eventually with physical stress your body gets used to it and moves on, or you figure out a way to make it work. By contrast, mental stress is harder to understand because my mind doesn't show indicators of stress. Like, with physical stress I'd notice, "Oh, I'm overworking, so my back hurts." My mind doesn't do that. My mind doesn't say, "Oh, the top right side of my brain hurts. I must be under mental stress."

Now that the mental stress is gone, it's changed all our staff meetings. Everyone in the office is more positive, especially me. I have a good team now because the other employees are willing to step up. I think I grew the respect from my guys from two things: One, a little bit of fear on their part. "If he's going to let his best friend go, then I'd better step up my game." Then two was, you know, "Man, he does really care about us and does listen to us."

Now that I'm looking back, I see not one thing negative has come out of that. Not one thing. Zero. So, if that helps on long term, do it because you're probably most likely right. You're most likely going to look back and be, like, "Why didn't I do this two years ago?" I just kept making excuses. And we've doubled our business since then. We have become so much more efficient and effective.

When *Can* You Hire Friends or Family?

Contribution by Aaron Miller

My daughter was actually one of the better employees I've ever had. She was sixteen or seventeen years old at the time. Basically, her job was a lot of clerical work, filing stuff, and creating forms. The forms that she created for me, I still use them today.

I wanted to make sure that she didn't report to me, that she report to somebody else. So, I didn't supervise her; I had my assistant supervise her. Because I knew she'd have another job somewhere else, it was important that she understand that she wasn't "just working for Dad.". . .

If my daughter wasn't doing the work, and that was never the case, but if she wasn't doing the work, then the lady that I had supervising her wouldn't have had any problems letting her know or letting me know if need be. She had the authority to do that.

I think if you're going to hire one of your children, ideally don't have them report to you. Give [whomever they're reporting to] the authority to supervise them like they would anybody else. It's not a good idea to give any special treatment to your children because that's going to be demoralizing to everybody else around. Because if you get somebody that can't do the work, that means everybody else has to pick up the work. That's going to cause problems down the road.

Firing someone is never easy, though it does become easier with practice. If there was a name you wrote down in chapter one of someone you know who needs to be let go from your company do not delay. Get your system in place to move them out, so that a superstar can move into that position and help your company soar.

Chapter 5: Employer Rights

Resources for employer rights are very limited. Most articles and sites are geared toward the rights of employees. The following is an article we've been given permission to include in this book. It is a very well-written, concise article outlining a few employer rights. The Appendix also has additional resources for employers.

Employers, Know Your Rights!

by Richard Tuschman, Board Certified Labor & Employment Attorney
SEP 18, 2012

Employment litigation has boomed in the last twenty years. Statutes such as the ADA and the FMLA have created new rights for employees. Decades-old laws such as Title VII (which prohibits many forms of discrimination) and the Fair Labor Standards Act (which sets the minimum wage and regulates overtime pay) remain popular among plaintiffs' lawyers and their clients. The cost of litigation has increased as well. Employers can spend $50,000 in attorney's fees defending even a baseless case. Naturally, you may be skittish about criticizing, much less terminating, your poorly performing employees. And you may be reluctant to ask your employees to sign agreements designed to protect your confidential business information.

Don't be. In today's ultracompetitive business environment, you cannot afford to retain poor performers. Nor can you afford to let employees take advantage of your hard work and intellectual property. Sure, employees have many legal rights. But as an employer, you too have rights. Here are just a few:

- *You have the right to demand hard work.* The law does not prohibit you from taking action against employees who are lazy or unproductive. Moreover, in most states you can require employees to work overtime, even weekends and holidays, provided that you pay your nonexempt employees the appropriate overtime wages. (Employees who are exempt as professionals, executives, administrators, and outside salespersons are not entitled to overtime compensation.) Weed out your unproductive employees and reward your hard workers with overtime pay when necessary.
- *You have the right to demand high-quality work.* Sloppy work product, poor customer service, and arguments with coworkers and supervisors are not legally protected workplace behaviors. Put an end to them through a system of progressive discipline.
- *You have the right to demand loyalty.* Employees do not have a right to solicit business for their own benefit or to set up a competing business while you employ them. You can and should terminate employees who put their own interests ahead of your business.
- *You have the right to be wrong.* Suppose you have reason to believe that an employee is stealing or otherwise not acting in the company's best interests, but you don't have conclusive proof. Fortunately the law does not require an employer to act like a prosecutor and obtain proof beyond a reasonable doubt. So as long as you act in good faith and without discrimination, you can lawfully act on your best available information, even if it turns out to be wrong.
- *You have the right to protect your trade secrets and confidential business information.* Many state laws protect against an employee's misappropriation of trade

secrets. But such statutes often define the term "trade secrets" narrowly. You should require employees who have access to customer lists, strategic plans, pricing information, financial data, and other confidential business information to sign confidentiality agreements that restrict their use of such information during their employment and after. State law also may allow you to require employees to sign agreements not to compete with your business or to solicit your customers for a period of time after their employment ends.

(Thank you Richard for allowing us to include your article.)

You may already know what the law prohibits you from doing as an employer. But knowing what the law *permits* you to do — and doing it — will improve the productivity of your workforce and give you an advantage over your competition.

Contribution by Alex Cantaboni

There's a thing called State, and the State doesn't care about employers. They really don't. They don't care that I've been threatened twice by employees. One time I had an employee threaten over the phone that he was going to shoot me if I went onto his personal property. The problem was that the employee had one of my work trucks that I needed for a different employee. So, I called the cops to see if they would go with me to get my work truck from the employee's home, you know, just to be on the safe side.

They said, "Has he threatened you?"

I said, "Yeah, over the phone."

The police then asked, "Well, did you actually see the gun?"

I said, "No, it was a verbal threat over the phone."

To which they replied, "Well, we can't do anything about it."

The Department of Labor doesn't care either, even if you have a witness. An employee can threaten you by saying, "You're a piece of crap. F you. I'm going to beat you up. I hate you," and there is nothing you can do about it. According to the Department of Labor, that's not a good enough reason for firing, which is sad.

Your rights as an employer and what you expect from your employees must clearly be stated in the policies manual. Take time to download the company policy outline from www.BBMMUSA.com/p/Hiring. Make sure every employee signs the manual and has a copy. It will solve so many employee problems.

Shoot for the Stars

Now you have the system for hiring superstars, and it is time to shoot for the stars by putting your ads out there and reeling them into your business. Keep in mind that, like my mentor Dan Kennedy says: "Eventually even your best racehorse goes lame," so you must always be hiring.

There are a lot of resources for you on our website that we have referred to in this book, and we encourage you to save yourself a ton of time and effort by going to our website and getting the downloads right now at www.BBMMUSA.com/p/Hiring . If you already have the downloads, good job, go ahead and make your life easier by using them with the tweaks you need to make them your own.

This book just scratches the surface of all there is to know about owning your own business and having the success you want. So, we have also included information on our website about standard operating procedures, financials, marketing, and obtaining the time freedom and financial freedom we business owners crave and strive for. So take advantage of all that information too. If you are truly serious about growing your business and want to be a part of our Mastermind that supports you and holds you accountable, then contact us directly www.BBMMUSA.com.

Appendix/Resources

1. How to Create an Effective Job Posting
   http://primepay.com/blog/9-elements-develop
   ing-good-job-description

2. How CEOs Spend Their Time
   https://www.slideshare.net/domo/
   how-ceos-spend-their-time-what-business-lead
   ers-do-in-an-average-day-53981103

3. How Effective CEOs Spend Their Time
   https://www.inc.com/john-mcdermott/jim-schleck
   ser-ceo-project-where-effective-ceos-spend-their-
   time.html

4. What to Do If Threatened at the Workplace by an
   Employee?
   http://woman.thenest.com/threatened-work
   place-employee-11749.html

5. What Constitutes a "Hostile Work Environment" or
   "Hostile Workplace?"
   http://www.toplawfirm.com/HostileWorkEnvironment
   .html

Contact the authors for free downloads or about participating in a Business Builders Mentor and Mastermind group by visiting www.BBMMUSA.com.